# CAKE
# Decorating
# TRICKS

# CAKE
# Decorating
# TRICKS

Clever ideas for creating fantastic cakes

SUE McMAHON

NEW HOLLAND

**Dedication**

I would like to dedicate this book to my father, Gerard McMahon, for his generous funding and support of all my hobbies, including sugarcraft.

Published in 2009 by
New Holland Publishers (UK) Ltd
London • Cape Town • Sydney • Auckland
www.newhollandpublishers.com

Garfield House, 86–88 Edgware Road, London W2 2EA, United Kingdom
80 McKenzie Street, Cape Town 8001, South Africa
Unit 1, 66 Gibbes Street, Chatswood, NSW 2067, Australia
218 Lake Road, Northcote, Auckland, New Zealand

ISBN 978 1 84773 285 9

EDITOR: Emma Pattison
EDITORIAL DIRECTION: Rosemary Wilkinson
DESIGN: Casebourne Rose Design Associates
PHOTOGRAPHY: Frank Wieder
PRODUCTION: Laurence Poos

Reproduction by Pica Digital, PTE Ltd, Singapore
Printed and bound by Times Offset (M) Sdn Bhd

# CONTENTS

# INTRODUCTION

Celebration cakes have grown in popularity over recent years, and the materials and equipment for making them at home have become more readily available. This book takes advantage of all the latest gadgets which will help you to achieve professional looking results as quickly as possible. No need to worry if you don't have a large selection of equipment – alternatives are given where possible, and most designs can be made from equipment that you are likely to already have in your kitchen.

This book starts with the basics of cake baking, because having a good base to decorate is extremely important, then covers the different types of icings and all the cake decorating tricks you will need to create stunning celebration cakes. Dip into the chapters to choose which effects you want to put together to create a truly unique finished design, and let your creativity flow!

Sue McMahon

# CHAPTER ONE

# BAKING CAKES

As well as looking good it's important that a cake should taste great, too. Spend a little time getting the cake base right and you will be rewarded later as a well-made cake base is much easier to decorate than a badly made one, and you won't have to spend time disguising flaws.

# Celebration Cakes

An important part of any celebration cake is the actual cake itself. Just as a house needs suitable foundations, when decorating a cake you need a suitable base cake. It's possible to make many different flavours of cakes with many different filling, but as this book concentrates mainly on the decoration, the actual cakes have been kept very simple with a choice of fruit cake or sponge cake in plain or chocolate varieties.

## Fruit Cake Basics

Fruit cakes are traditionally used for wedding cakes and Christmas cakes. As the cake is very rich and packed full of fruit, the cakes will keep for a long time; fruit cakes can be made about 2–3 months before they are needed so they have time to to mature. Often alcohol such as brandy or rum is spooned over them which further helps to preserve them. Traditionally the top tier of a wedding cake is saved to be used for the Christening of the first child, although this seems to be less common today, particularly as sponge cakes are becoming more popular for wedding cakes. The biggest advantage of fruit cakes is that they can be decorated in advance, which can save any last minute stress.

## Sponge Cake Basics

Children generally prefer sponge cakes to fruit cakes, and so children's birthday cakes are usually sponge cakes. When a cake is going to be decorated it needs to be a fairly solid cake to be able to support the weight of the icing, and a Madeira-type cake works well. If all the ingredients are at room temperature, it's very quick to make a Madeira cake using the 'all in one' method, where all of the ingredients are tipped into a bowl and beaten together until smooth.

Substituting some of the flour for cocoa powder will give a good-flavoured chocolate cake, and the plain and chocolate varieties have been used for the cakes in this book. You can of course adapt the recipes for different flavours; for example you could use some strong coffee in place of the milk in the chocolate cake for a mocha cake, or you can add a few chopped or ground nuts to vary the flavour.

# Preparing the Cake Tin

Before making the cake mixture, prepare the cake tin so that it's ready to use. This is particularly important when making sponge cakes with self-raising flour. The raising agents in the flour start to work when the flour becomes wet as well as when heated, so as soon as the flour has been mixed with the liquid ingredients (such as the eggs and milk) the raising agents start to work. If the cake is left unbaked for a while then it won't rise well when it is put in the oven.

If the cake tin is a simple shape, such as a round or a square, then the easiest way to prepare the tin is to line it with baking parchment. Once the cake is baked it will then be easy to remove the cake from the tin, and the paper also protects the tin so it will be easy to clean.

## Lining a Round Tin

**1.** Place the cake tin on a double layer of baking parchment and draw around the base of the tin. Cut out the 2 circles of paper, making them slightly smaller than the tin (so they will fit into the base of the tin). To line the sides of the tin, place the cake tin on baking parchment and roll the paper around the tin, and then cut the paper so it overlaps slightly.

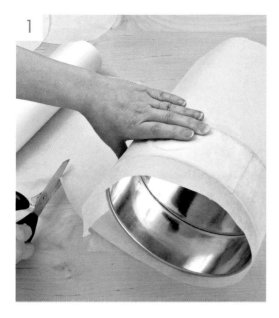

**2.** Fold the paper in half lengthways, then fold up the cut edges about 3 cm (1¹⁄₃ in) and press down well to make a crease. Use scissors to make lots of snips along along the long edges, to just beyond the creased line.

**3.** Fit the long strip around the sides of the tin, pressing the folded and snipped edge in well around the base, so that it follows the shape of the tin. Place the 2 circles of baking parchment in the base of the tin.

## tip

If you have a recipe for a round cake and want to bake it in a square tin, use a square tin which is 2.5 cm (1 in) smaller that the round tin size. For example, the recipe for a 23 cm (9 in) round cake could also be used to make a 20 cm (8 in) square cake. Halving the quantities given for the 23 cm (9 in) round recipe will make a 12.5 cm (5 in) square cake or doubling the quantities will be sufficient for a 28 cm (11 in) square cake.

## Lining a Square Tin

**1.** Cut out 2 squares of baking parchment for the base as for Lining a Round Tin (page 11). Cut a strip to go around the sides of the tin and fold it in half, and then fold up the cut sides so the paper is just higher than the tin. Fold over one end of the strip and then place the strip inside the tin. Fold it so it's the length of one side of the tin and repeat the folds 4 times.

**2.** Use scissors to cut out a 'V' shape from the folded up edge at each of the sides of the tin.

**3.** Fit the lining paper into the sides of the tin, making sure it goes right into the corners. Place the 2 squares of parchment paper in the base of the tin.

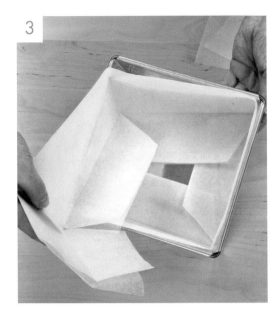

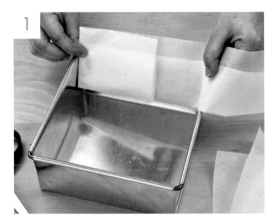

## tip

Look out for flexible silicone moulds that don't need greasing. After baking, just peel away the silicone to leave smooth-surfaced cakes. Silicone moulds are also easier to clean after use than metal tins.

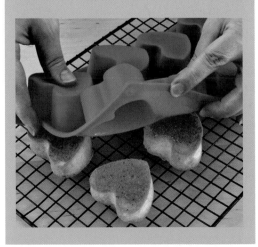

## tip

Try using re-usable silicone liners for lining mini cake tins. After baking the liners can be easily peeled off the cakes leaving a smooth and crumb-free surface.

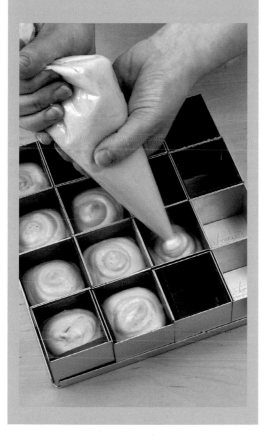

## Cake Quantities

The quantities given for both the fruit cake and sponge cakes will make a 23 cm (9 in) round cake. If you're making a 3-tier wedding cake, then good proportions to have for the tiers are 18 cm (6 in), 23 cm (9 in) and 30 cm (12 in). Halve the quantities of the recipe for the 23 cm (9 in) round to make an 18 cm (6 in) round cake, and double the quantities to make a 30 cm (12 in) round cake.

## Fruit Cake

This recipe can be varied depending on which types of dried fruits you prefer. Some luxury dried fruit mixes contain cherries and exotic dried fruits, whereas others are plainer (and cheaper). Alternatively you can make your own mix by using a selection of currants, raisins, sultanas and mixed peel. For a tropical cake, try chopping finely some dried ready-to-eat pineapple and papaya.

## Preparing an Irregular Shape Tin

When it's not possible to line a tin with baking parchment, the tin may be brushed with melted butter and then coated with a little flour. Or you could brush the tin with a proprietary brand of greasing mix, which greases and flours the tin at the same time, using a silicone brush so the bristles don't come off on the tin.

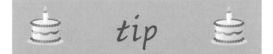

## tip

To help ensure a really smooth surface on a fruit cake use a wet hand to press the mixture down until it's flat. The top of the cake can get quite wet as any excess water will evaporate during cooking.

## Making a Fruit Cake

300 g (10 oz) butter, softened
300 g (10 oz) soft dark brown sugar
1 tablespoon black treacle
2 level teaspoons ground mixed spice
1 level teaspoon ground ginger
6 large eggs
350 g (12 oz) plain flour
100 g (3½ oz) ground almonds
1.25 kg (2 lb) dried mixed fruit
23 cm (9 in) round or 20 cm (8 in) square
cake tin, lined with baking parchment

**1.** Set the oven to 150°C/300°F/Gas Mark 2.

**2.** Place the butter, sugar, black treacle, mixed spice and ginger in a bowl and beat until the mixture is light and fluffy.

**3.** Beat in 1 egg at a time, adding a small spoonful of flour with each egg to help prevent the mixture curdling. Beat in the remaining flour and ground almonds, then fold in the dried mixed fruit.

**4.** Spoon the mixture into the lined cake tin and level the surface.

**5.** Bake the cake in the centre of the oven for 3–3½ hours, or until the cake feels firm to the touch in the centre and a skewer comes out clean.

**6.** Remove the cake from the oven and place the tin on a wire rack. Leave the cake to cool completely in the tin before removing it and either decorating it or preparing it for storing.

## tip

To help prevent a fruit cake from drying out during baking, particularly in a fan oven, place a roasting tin of hot water on the oven shelf below the cake. This will create a steamy atmosphere during cooking, helping to keep the cake moist.

wrap the cake totally in baking parchment, then wrap it in foil.

**2.** Fold the ends of the foil over to exclude as much air as possible and then store the cake in a cool, dry place. Label the cake with the date, so that you don't forget when it was made.

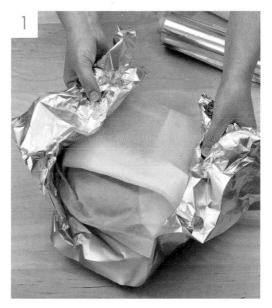

## Preserving Fruit Cakes

Spooning alcohol such as brandy or rum over a fruit cake will help to preserve it. Make sure a spirit is used which will act as a preservative. Drinks with a lower alcohol content, such as wine, may cause the cake to ferment. Spooning the alcohol over the cake while the cake is slightly warm will mean that it is absorbed into the cake more quickly than when the cake is cold. However remember to leave the cake to cool in the tin to ensure that the sides remain straight.

## Storing Fruit Cakes

A fruit cake will keep for up to 3 months providing it is wrapped and stored correctly. Make sure the cake is completely cold before wrapping it otherwise condensation will form inside the wrapping paper and the cake may go mouldy as a result .

**1.** Make sure the cake is completely cold before packing it for storage. For fruit cakes,

# Sponge Cake

Sponge cakes can be made using a wide-variety of flavours. Below are recipes for plain and chocolate sponges, which can easily be adapted to make coffee or lemon cakes.

## Making a Plain Sponge Cake

350 g (12 oz) butter, softened
350 g (12 oz) caster sugar
500 g (1 lb) self-raising flour
6 large eggs
6 tablespoons milk
Few drops vanilla extract
23 cm (9 in) round or 20 cm (8 in) square cake tin, lined with baking parchment

**1.** Set the oven to 160°C/325°F/Gas Mark 3.

**2.** Place the butter, sugar and flour in a bowl and add the eggs, milk and vanilla

*tip*

The easiest way to fill small-size cake tins or moulds is to pipe the cake mixture into them. Fill a large disposable piping bag with the cake mixture, cut off the end of the bag to give a large hole and then pipe the mixture into the tin or mould, re-filling the bag as necessary.

extract to taste. Beat until the mixture is smooth.

**3.** Spoon the mixture into the lined cake tin. Bake the cake in the centre of the oven for $1^{1}/_{2}$–$1^{3}/_{4}$ hours, or until the cake has risen and feels firm to the touch in the centre. As an extra check, insert a skewer into the centre of the cake – if it comes out clean the cake is cooked, but if there is any mixture on the skewer then the cake isn't cooked and will need to stay in the oven for a little longer.

**4.** Remove the cake from the oven and leave it to cool in the tin for 15–20 minutes, then transfer it to a wire rack to cool completely.

## Making a Chocolate Sponge Cake

350 g (12 oz) butter, softened
350 g (12 oz) caster sugar
450 g (15 oz) self-raising flour
50 g (1$^{3}/_{4}$ oz) cocoa powder
6 large eggs
6 tablespoons milk
Few drops vanilla extract
23 cm (9 in) round or 20 cm (8 in) square cake tin, lined with baking parchment

Follow the method and baking times as for the Plain Sponge Cake above, adding the cocoa powder for a chocolate flavour.

## Storing the Cake

The cake will keep for 3–4 days stored in an airtight container. If the cake needs to be kept for longer it may be wrapped in baking parchment and then foil, or in a freezer bag, and frozen for up to 3 months. Allow the cake to defrost thoroughly at room temperature before decorating.

# Irregular Shape Tins

If you have an irregular shape tin and want to know how much mixture to use, pour water into tin to the depth that the cake mixture should fill and then measure the quantity of water by pouring it into a measuring jug. The cake mixture will rise slightly, but it's easier to measure the tin to the height that you'd like the cake to be, and if the cake is too deep it can always be trimmed slightly.

The Fruit Cake recipe on page 14 makes about 2 litres (3½ pints), so, for example, if the tin takes 1 litre (1½ pints) water, then use half the quantities given in the recipe.

The Plain Sponge recipe on page 16 and the Chocolate Sponge recipe on page 16 both make about 1.5 litres (2½ pints), and so recipes can be converted accordingly. The volume of the sponge recipe is less than the fruit cake as sponge cakes rises more during cooking and has a spongy texture, whereas the fruit cake is denser.

baking cakes

# Levelling a Domed Cake

**1.** If a cake has risen in the centre then the easiest way to level it is to remove it from the tin, place a cake drum under it and then return it to the tin so that the dome sticks up above the rim of the tin.

**2.** Use a long-bladed knife to cut the dome off, keeping the knife against the cake tin to ensure that the cut is level.

**3.** Remove the domed piece of cake and discard (or eat) it.

baking cakes

Cakes don't always have to be baked in traditional cake tins. They can be baked in other ovenproof containers too, such as heat-proof glass bowls or even flowerpots. If using flowerpots always use new pots, scrub them well before use and make sure that they are fully lined with baking parchment (this is important as it will ensure that the cake mixture does not come into contact with the clay pot).

# CHAPTER TWO

# COVERING CAKES

If you can roll out pastry you can also ice a cake. Both marzipan and sugarpaste coverings simply require kneading to soften them, then they can be rolled out and lifted over the cake, pressed gently in place and then polished to give a smooth surface. Easy!

# Working with Marzipan and Sugarpaste

Covering cakes with marzipan then sugarpaste is a common way of decorating fruit cakes. The marzipan seals the cake so that none of the juices seep through and discolour the icing. However, for anyone with a nut allergy, sugarpaste may be applied straight onto a nut-free fruit cake, but the cake will not keep as long as if it had the protecting layer of marzipan.

Sponge cakes may be covered with both marzipan and sugarpaste, or the marzipan layer may be omitted. Using marzipan will give a smoother surface, but it saves time and it's less expensive to leave it out.

It's easier to work with ready-made marzipan and sugarpaste, rather than making them at home from scratch. There are several manufacturers of very reliable products that always give consistent results, and any left-overs from the shop-bought versions seem to keep for longer than home-made marzipan and sugarpaste.

Both products need to be kneaded well before use so that they are soft enough to roll out. Kneading the products well before rolling them out will also help to prevent them from cracking. When kneading the products make sure that your work surface is clean and free of icing sugar, then when rolling them out dust the surface lightly with icing sugar to help prevent the paste from sticking. Don't use icing sugar when kneading either marzipan or sugarpaste as the sugar will dry the products out and they may crack during use.

## Preparing the Cake

**1.** To stick the marzipan to a fruit or sponge cake the cake needs to be spread with a thin layer of apricot glaze that will act as the 'glue'. If you're unable to buy apricot glaze then use smooth apricot jam, or sieve traditional apricot jam.

**2.** Upturn the cake and place it centrally on a cake drum. Bring some apricot glaze to the boil and then brush the glaze over the top and sides of the cake. It's a good idea to use a silicone brush rather than a traditional pastry brush as stray bristles can stick to the glaze.

covering cakes

## Covering a Cake with Marzipan

**1.** Knead the marzipan to soften it, and then roll it out onto a surface lightly dusted with icing sugar. To ensure the marzipan is of an even thickness, roll it between spacer bars, rolling until the rolling pin is touching the bars.

**2.** Lift the marzipan over the cake and then press it down over the top and against the sides, easing in any fullness so that there aren't any creases in the marzipan on the sides of the cake.

**3.** Use a small sharp knife to trim away any excess marzipan around the base of the cake.

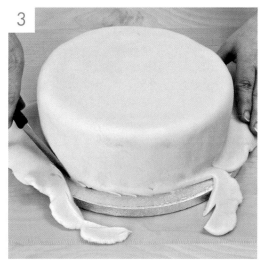

## tip

To get a really smooth surface rub over the top and sides of the cake with an icing smoother. This will help to remove any bumps and finger marks.

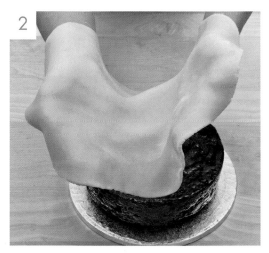

## Covering a Cake with Sugarpaste

**1.** Knead the sugarpaste to soften it. It's ready when there aren't any cracks in the surface, and when the surface feels smooth and satin-like. Roll the sugarpaste out on a surface lightly dusted with icing sugar. If there are any air bubbles then pierce them with a needle (it's easier to get rid of them when the sugarpaste is flat, rather than when it's on the cake).

**2.** Brush water over the marzipan. It's best to boil some water and leave it to cool rather than using water straight from the tap.

**3.** Lift the sugarpaste over the cake and press it down on the top and then the sides, smoothing it over the marzipan. Make sure that no air is trapped between the marzipan and sugarpaste otherwise the sugarpaste will bubble up. If there are any bubbles pierce them with a needle and rub over the hole so that it's not visible. Use a small knife to trim away the sugarpaste, either at the base of the cake or, for a professional look, trim around the edge of the cake drum so that the top of the cake drum is covered too. To get the surface really smooth polish it with an icing smoother, as for the marzipan.

2

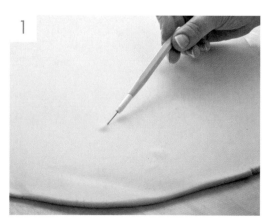

1

3

**4.** If the sugarpaste on the board looks uneven then roll it with a textured frilling tool, pressing it into the soft sugarpaste and rolling it slightly forwards and backwards. Lift the tool up, move slightly around the board and repeat until you have moved all the way around the board. This not only evens out the sugarpaste but also gives a really professional finish to your cake.

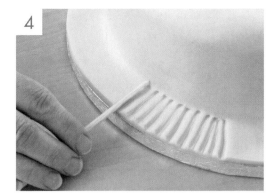

## tip

Adding a ribbon to the edge of the cake drum gives an instant professional-looking finish. Use either double-sided sticky tape or a glue stick to attach the ribbon in place.

# CHAPTER THREE

# SOFT ICINGS

The icings in this chapter can be categorised as 'soft icings' as they are soft to work with, can be spread over cakes with a palette knife and used to pipe decorations. If you are covering a cake with royal icing remember to add some glycerine to it to keep it soft and prevent it from becoming very hard as it dries.

# Royal Icing and Buttercream

Both royal icing and buttercream can be used to cover cakes as well as for piping decorations. Royal icing can be used to completely cover fruit cakes, such as wedding cakes – just cover the cake with marzipan first to seal the cake, then apply the royal icing in thin layers as for covering a cake with buttercream, allowing the layers to dry before putting on the next. When a cake has been iced with royal icing or sugarpaste then any decorative piping is usually also done in royal icing, and if the cake has been covered in buttercream then the piping is done in buttercream too.

## Quick Buttercream

This buttercream is quicker to make than Swiss Meringue Buttercream (see page 29), but as the sugar crystals are not dissolved it doesn't have the same smooth texture. This type of buttercream will crust over, so once it's made, press a sheet of cling-film over the surface until you are ready use it.

### Making Quick Buttercream

*Sufficient to fill and cover a 23 cm (9 in)
round or 20 cm (8 in) square cake*
500 g (1 lb) icing sugar
250 g (8 oz) unsalted butter, softened
2–3 tablespoons boiling water
Few drops vanilla extract
Pinch of salt

**1.** Tip the icing sugar into a bowl and add the butter and boiling water.

**2.** Beat the icing until smooth, preferably in a table-top food mixer.

*tip*

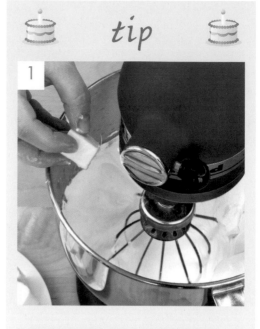

**1.** When making Swiss Meringue Buttercream the mixture may appear to curdle when the butter is first added to the meringue.

**2.** Don't panic if this happens. Simply continue whisking the mixture and it will combine to give a smooth buttercream.

soft icings

**3.** Add vanilla extract and salt taste.

**4.** Cover the buttercream with a sheet of cling film until you are ready to use it, and if necessary re-whisk it before use if it has become too thick.

## Swiss Meringue Buttercream

Swiss meringue buttercream has a very smooth texture and gives cakes a professional finish. The best way to make this buttercream is by using a table-top mixer, as the mixture needs a lot of whisking which would be difficult to do by hand.

## Making Swiss Meringue Buttercream

*Sufficient to fill and cover a 23 cm (9 in) round or 20 cm (8 in) square cake*
4 medium egg whites
300 g (10 oz) caster sugar
450 g (15 oz) butter, softened
Few drops vanilla extract
Pinch of salt

**1.** Place the egg whites and sugar in a bowl and place the bowl over a pan of simmering water. Stir the mixture gently until the sugar dissolves, then remove the bowl from the heat.

**2.** Whisk the egg white and sugar until the mixture has cooled and resembles a thick and frothy meringue, then gradually whisk in the butter. Whisk the mixture until smooth. Add vanilla extract and salt to taste.

**3.** The buttercream is ready to use immediately but may be stored in the fridge for 3–4 days. It will need to come to room temperature and be re-whisked before use.

## Filling and Covering a Cake with Buttercream

Buttercream filling and coating is perfect for sponge cakes. As well as filling a cake with a layer of buttercream, a layer of jam is often spread over a plain sponge cake to add extra flavour. The sides of the cake may be left plain, or coated in chocolate vermicelli or finely chopped nuts.

**1.** Cut the sponge cake in half using a serrated long-bladed knife, such as a bread knife. Keeping the knife level with 2 even supports, such as upturned glass bowls, will ensure that the cut is even. Just move the knife supports (or bowls) as required while cutting through the cake.

soft icings

**2.** Remove the top half of the cake and spread jam over one half and buttercream over the other half.

**3.** Place the half which was the top of the cake on a cake drum, then place the other half on top to sandwich the filling in the middle (placing the half of the cake which was on top when the cake was baked on the bottom will ensure a totally flat top to the cake).

**4.** Use a small palette knife to smooth around the edges and remove any excess buttercream that may have oozed out when the layers are sandwiched together.

**5.** Spread buttercream on the top of the cake and use an icing ruler held at a 45° angle to smooth the icing. An icing ruler is ideal for this job as they are usually made from metal and so won't flex. If you don't have an icing ruler a strong, non-flexible ordinary plastic or metal ruler may be used instead.

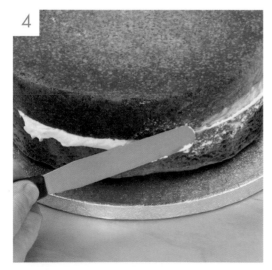

soft icings

**6.** Use a small palette knife to remove any excess buttercream from the top of the cake.

**7.** Cover the sides of the cake with buttercream. The easiest way to achieve a smooth finish is to place the cake on a turntable and spread buttercream over the sides of the cake. Then, holding a side scraper at a 45° to the cake, spin the cake around on the turntable, trying to turn it in just one movement, while keeping the side scraper in the same position. Take away the side scraper with any excess buttercream.

**8.** Remove the excess buttercream from the top edge of the cake using a small palette knife.

**9.** To coat the sides of the cake, tip some vermicelli onto a sheet of baking parchment. Hold the cake in one hand and tilt it slightly. Use the other hand to scoop up the vermicelli and press it against the sides of the cake. Turn the cake to cover all the sides. Tap the cake drum lightly on the work surface to shake off any excess.

**10.** Pipe swirls of buttercream around the top edge of the cake. Pipe swirls dividing the cake into 4 and then fill-in the gaps between the swirls to help ensure that the swirls are evenly placed.

**11.** Press a chocolate decoration, such as the Quick Chocolate Stars on page 62, into each swirl.

## Royal Icing

Royal icing is the classic wedding cake covering, and should be snowy white in colour. The recipe below is ideal for making decorations such as Piped Flowers (page 96), but if the icing is going to be used to cover the cake you will need to add about 1 tablespoon glycerine for each 500 g (1 lb) icing sugar to help keep the icing soft enough to cut. If glycerine is not added then the icing will be very hard and will need to be chiselled off the cake!

## Making Royal Icing

*Sufficient to fill and cover a 23 cm (9 in)
round or 20 cm (8 in) square cake*
3 large egg whites
Approximately 750 g (1 ½ lb) icing sugar
1 tablespoon glycerine (optional)

**1.** Lightly beat the egg whites to break them down, preferably using the paddle beater from a table-top mixer. Gradually beat in the icing sugar. Add enough icing sugar to thicken the mixture, then beat using the slowest speed of an electric mixer for about 10 minutes until the icing is light and fluffy.

### tip

To save time when making royal icing, look out for Royal Icing Sugar, which is a mixture of icing sugar and powdered egg white. Just add water and it's ready to use.

soft icings

**2.** Adjust the consistency, if necessary, by either adding more icing sugar if it's too runny or a few drops of water if it's too stiff. Beat for at least 2–3 minutes after each addition of icing sugar to check the consistency.

**3.** When the icing has reached the desired consistency beat in the glycerine, if using.

**4.** The surface of the icing will form a crust quite quickly, so as soon as the icing has been made press a sheet of cling film against the surface of the icing, then cover the bowl with a damp cloth. The icing will keep for up to 2 days, as long as the cloth covering it is kept damp. The icing should be stored in a cool place, but not in the fridge. If it becomes too soft simply re-beat before use.

soft icings

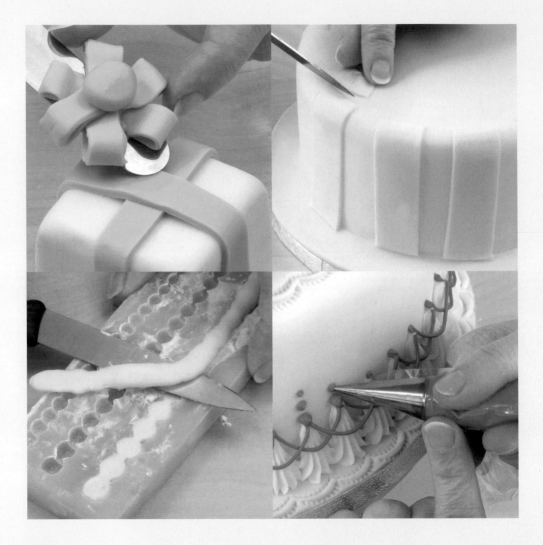

# CHAPTER FOUR

# BASIC DECORATIONS

Once the cake has been baked and covered in icing then the creative part of cake decorating can begin, and the cake can be personalised with an appropriate design. From simple piped borders and moulded pearls to ropes and tassels, the combinations of designs are almost endless and can achieve subtle textures or bright colours depending on the occasion.

# Decorating Techniques

As well as thinking about the top decoration for a cake, it's important to think about the sides of the cake too. If time is short, try crimping or embossing sugarpaste, and don't just look at cake decorating equipment as a wide variety of craft embossers will work on cakes – just make sure they are very clean if they have been used for other projects! Piping with royal icing or buttercream is a traditional way of decorating the sides of a cake, but don't worry if piping is not your thing, as there are now a wide variety of moulds available so you no longer have to have a steady hand as the moulds will produce neat and even edgings for cakes. It's even possible to decorate a cake without ever using a piping bag.

## Crimping

A very quick way to pattern the edge of the cake covered in sugarpaste is to use a crimper. Crimping is also a very good way of disguising any uneven edges and will add pattern to the cake without you having to mix-up any other icing, so it's an almost instant decoration. Crimpers need to be used as soon as the cake has been covered with sugarpaste, while the sugarpaste is still soft. Crimpers are a bit like tweezers and come with a variety of different patterned ends. The secret to attractive crimping is to ensure the pattern looks the same all the way around the cake. It doesn't matter if it's done lightly and with only a little pressure, or if it is thick and heavy, as long as each crimp looks the same. Make sure that the crimpers are clean and dry; if they are damp they will stick to the sugarpaste.

## tip

Crimping around the edge of the cake drum is a great way of disguising any unevennes in the thickness of the sugarpaste, and it looks great too.

### Simple Crimping

**1.** Hold the crimpers slightly apart and press them into the sugarpaste. Squeeze the crimpers together, then release the pressure and lift the crimpers away from the icing.

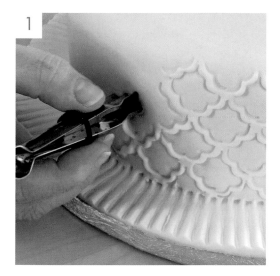

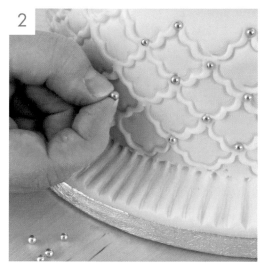

## Decorative Crimping

**1.** Start with a layer of crimping around the bottom of the cake, holding the crimpers alternately to the right and then to the left. It's important to get the first bottom layer even, as the other layers are worked up from the bottom layer to the top of the cake.

**2.** To add extra decoration, silver balls may be pressed into the sugarpase at the points where the crimping lines meet. If they are stuck on as soon as the cake has been crimped, the sugarpaste should still be soft enough to hold them, but if the sugarpaste has dried too much it may be necessary to pipe a little royal icing where each ball is to be stuck.

## Embossing

Embossing is a technique that works well on cakes which have been covered with sugarpaste – just remember to use embossers as soon as the cake has been covered as the sugarpaste needs to be soft.

It's possible to buy all sorts of designs of embossers from cake decorating supply shops, but look out for other items that will

also work well. The handle of a fancily-decorated tea-spoon or even an elaborate dress ring can be pressed into soft sugarpaste to emboss the surface.

## Craft Embossers

**1.** Try using a paint-stamping tool as an embosser. As well as using it to texture the sides of the cake it can also be used around the edge of the cake drum.

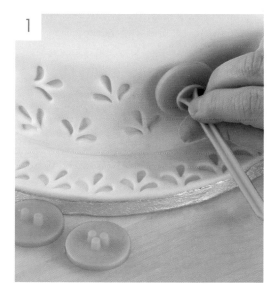

basic decorations

## Tile Spacers

**1.** Try looking in DIY stores for inspiration. Plastic tile spacers can be used for embossing. Generally spacers for floor tiles are diagonal criss-crosses, whereas wall tile spacers are in square grids. Press the tile spacer into the sugarpaste, pressing at in one end, and then work along the spacer pressing it so that it follows the shape of the cake.

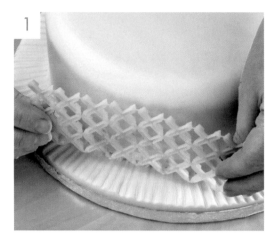

**2.** Remove the spacer. Check that all the ridges have embossed. If any are missing, break off one tile spacer and press it to fill in any missed spaces or gaps.

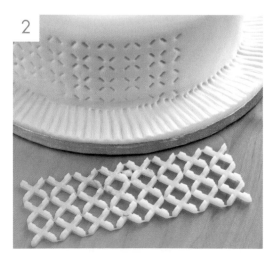

## Textured Cutters

Specialist lace-effect cutters may be purchased from cake decorating supply stores. These cutters come in a set with a cutter for the basic outline shape, plus several different embossing designs.

**1.** Choose the embosser design to be used. Knead some sugarpaste to soften it and then roll it out thinly on a surface lightly dusted with icing sugar. Press the embosser into the sugarpaste and cut along the base of the cutter and at either side to the length of the cutter, then lift the embosser off the sugarpaste.

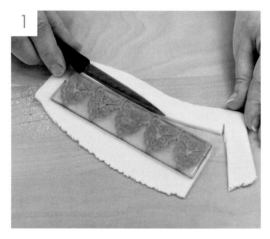

**2.** Line the cutter up with the embossed design, and then cut along the fancy edge.

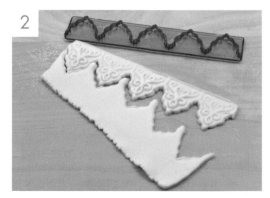

basic decorations

**3.** Brush some water onto the back of the embossed lace piece and stick it onto the cake. Press it lightly into place, taking care not to press-out the embossed design.

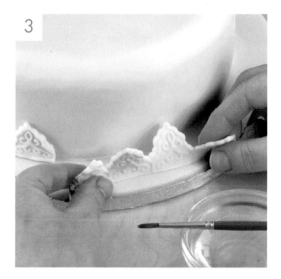

**4.** Two pieces of the embossed lace design may be placed side-by-side, such as around the top edge of a cakeor the sides, to give a wider lace border.

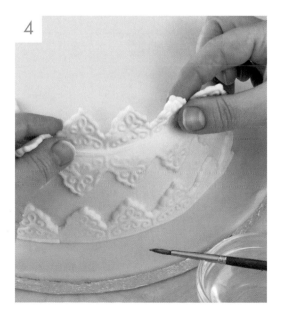

## tip

Sometimes using a knife to cut sugarpaste can cause the shape to become distorted. If this happens try using a pizza wheel to give a smooth, clean cut.

## Stripes

**1.** Roll out some sugarpaste thinly on a surface lightly dusted with icing sugar and cut it into strips.

**2.** Cut one end of each strip to give a smooth edge. Paint some water onto the back of the strips and stick them against the sides of the cakes with equal distance between them and

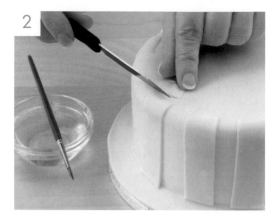

with the cut edge at the base. Cut away any excess at the top of the strips so that they are all the same height.

## Moulded Borders

It's possible to buy various designs of soft silicone moulds which are suitable for using to make borders such as lace designs, ropes and pearls. Using moulds will give consistently-sized decorations, which can be very useful if you have lots of decorations to make, particularly for tiered wedding cakes.

### String of Pearls

**1.** If the mould has several different sizes of pearls, choose which one to use and dust that section with cornflour.

**2.** Roll a long sausage-shape of sugarpaste, just thicker than the pearls.

**3.** Open up the mould slightly by bending the sides of it back and place the sausage of sugarpaste into the mould.

**4.** Press the sugarpaste down well into the mould. Use a small sharp knife to cut away

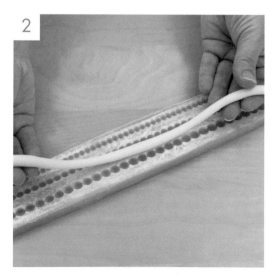

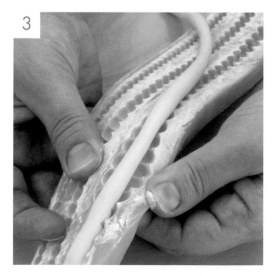

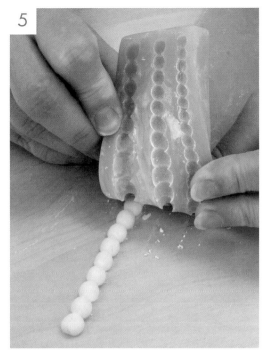

the excess sugarpaste from the top of the mould.

**5.** Peel the mould back to release the string of pearls.

**6.** Brush some water onto the cake where the pearls are to go, then carefully lift the strand of pearls and stick them into place. If liked, they may be dusted with some lustre colour before sticking them onto the cake to make them appear even more pearl-like.

41

## Piped Borders

The classic way of decorating cakes is to pipe patterns, which can be varied depending on the size and design of the piping tube that is used. Piping works well using either royal icing or buttercream. Generally, if a cake is covered in royal icing or sugarpaste then the designs are piped using royal icing, and if the cake is covered in buttercream then the borders are also piped in buttercream.

If royal icing is used it needs to be soft enough to allow the piping bag to be squeezed so that the icing will come out easily. However, it also needs to be firm enough to hold it's shape as the icing dries; if it's too soft the design will collapse before it dries. As these designs are piped all the way around the cake it's easier if the cake is placed on an icing turntable, although this isn't essential as you can just turn the cake around when working on it.

### Snailstrail

To create a simple and delicate border pipe a design know as a snailstrail around the base of the cake. Use a plain writing tube, such as a No. 2 plain tube, and fill a piping bag with icing. As the piping tube only has a small hole it won't need a lot of icing, so don't overfill the bag. Rest the piping tube against the side of the cake and gently squeeze the piping bag to form a ball of icing. Stop the pressure on the piping bag, but keep the point in the icing, and then take the bag to one side. If you're right-handed then it's easier to work anticlockwise around the cake, so take the piping tube to the right, and the opposite way if you're left-handed. Repeat the piping of the balls to give a beaded design around the end of the cake.

### Shell

A shell border is piped in the same way as the snailstrail, but using a shell piping tube instead of the plain piping tube. As shell piping tubes are usually bigger than writing piping tubes it's necessary to put more icing into the piping bag.

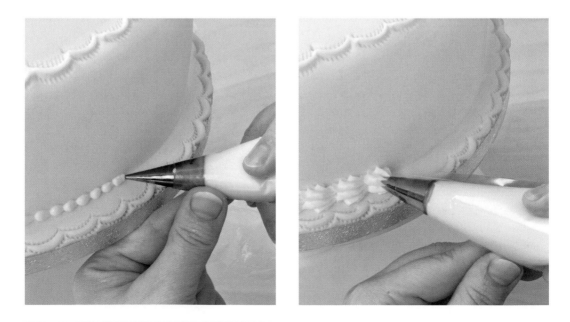

## Drop Loop Border

**1.** Instead of piping shells around the base of a cake, pipe each shell separately, piping them vertically. It's easier to do this if the cake is on a tilting turntable, but otherwise put something solid like a book under the front edge of the cake to tilt it. If using royal icing, leave the icing to dry.

**2.** Fill a piping bag fitted with a writing piping tube (e.g. No. 2) with coloured icing

and pipe dropped loops between the tips of alternate stars.

**3.** Pipe a second layer of dropped loops between the first layer, keeping all the loops hanging at the same level.

**4.** Pipe 3 dots in decreasing sizes from the point of each star, going up towards the top of the cake.

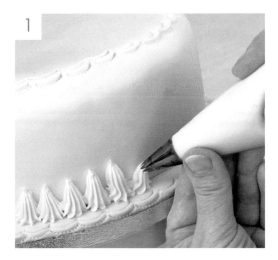

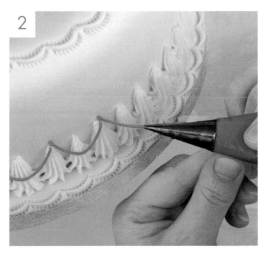

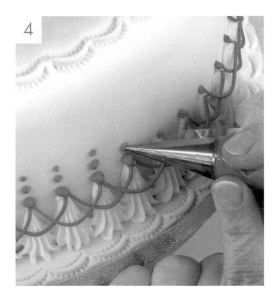

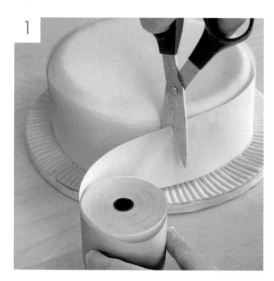

## Marking Scallops

**1.** Wrap a strip of till roll around a cake and cut it to the right length.

**2.** Fold the paper into the required number of sections, then fold the paper in half and cut out a half-scallop. When the strip is opened out again there will be the required number of even scallops.

**3.** Pin the strip of paper around the cake. Use large-headed pins to help ensure that they don't get mislaid. Wipe the points of the pins with an antibacterial wash and allow them to dry before using them and make sure that they only go into the icing and not into the cake. Take great care to ensure they are removed from the cake as soon as they are finished with. Use a scribing tool or a pin to mark the lines of the scallops.

## Ropes

Ropes look good when evenly-spaced around a cake, so mark the cake into scallops as described above. As well as putting a rope in scallops on the sides, try a rope around the base of the cake too.

---

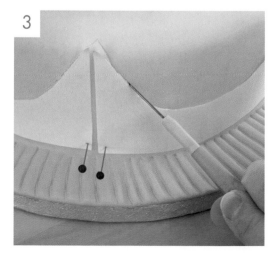

**1.** Knead some sugarpaste to soften it, then work some white vegetable fat into it to make it really soft.

**2.** To make even ropes, use a sugar shaper with the disc that looks like 3 interlinking circles. Carefully fit the disc onto the base of the shaper.

**3.** Roll a piece of sugarpaste into a sausage shape and place it in the chamber of the sugar shaper, then screw the top of the shaper firmly back in place.

**4.** Squeeze the lever on the side of the shaper to extrude the sugarpaste. Squeeze until all of the sugarpaste has come out of the chamber.

basic decorations

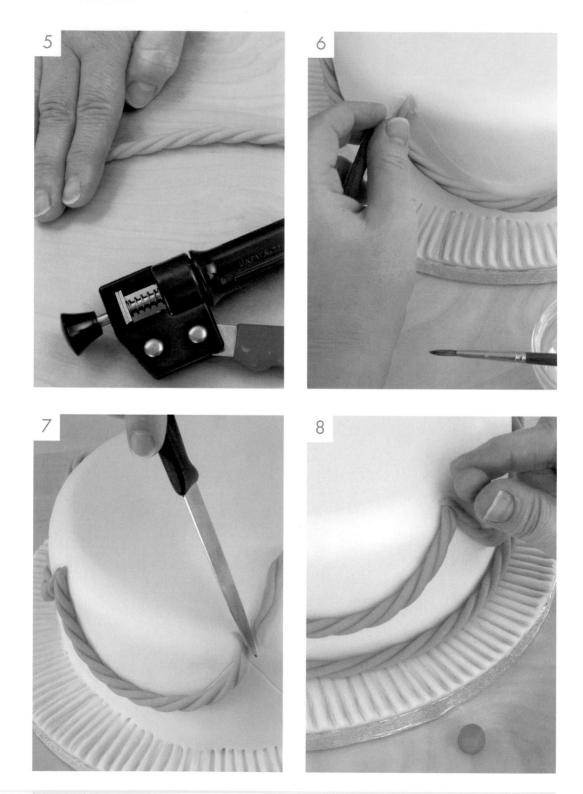

basic decorations

**5.** Roll either end of the sugarpaste so that it twists into a rope.

**6.** Brush a line of water over one of the scallops and then lift the rope and stick it into place.

**7.** Cut off the ends of the rope using a small knife, at the top of the scallops.

**8.** Roll small balls of sugarpaste, brush some water onto the backs of them and then stick one at the top of each scallop to cover the joins in the ropes.

**9.** If there is also a rope around the base of the cake make sure the joins are directly beneath the points of the scallops, then place small balls of sugarpaste under each scallop to hide the joins.

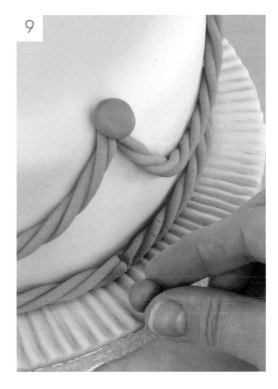

9

*tip*

If you don't have a sugar shaper you can roll-out two long pieces of sugarpaste by hand until they are sausage-shaped and then twist them together to make a rope. The rope can then be stuck onto the cake as described above.

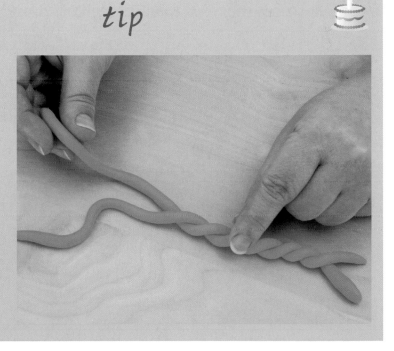

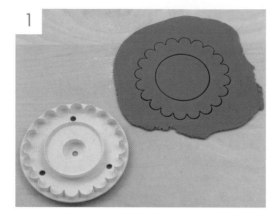

## Frills

**1.** Roll out some sugarpaste thinly on a surface lightly dusted with icing sugar and cut out a frill using a frill cutter.

**2.** Roll around the fluted edge with a cocktail stick, taking care not to stretch the inside plain edge. Cut into the frill so that it becomes a strip.

**3.** Paint a line of water over one of the scallops and place a cocktail stick at the top two points of a scallop. Carefully lift the frill up and press it over the painted line.

 *tip*

In general it looks good to have 6 frills around a cake. To ensure the frills are positioned correctly mark the cake into 6 scallops as described on page 44 before you begin making the frills. The frills above are made using a round frill cutter, but if you don't have one try using a fluted biscuit cutter and a smaller plain round cutter. To prevent the frills from loosing their shape as they dry cocktail sticks can be used as supports. Although it is often said that nothing should be inserted into a cake, cocktail sticks are sold for food use so they are safe to use in cakes. They are also large enough that they won't accidentally become lost and be eaten by mistake. Just make sure that they only go into the icing and don't pierce the cake.

basic decorations

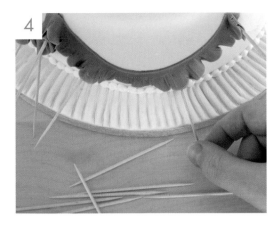

**4.** Place cocktail sticks under the frill to lift the frill up and press the sticks into the sugarpaste. Cut off any excess frill at the ends. Repeat the frills all around the cake.

**5.** For the top frill, cut out a frill in the same colour sugarpaste as the cake covering and frill it in the same way as the base frill. Before cutting it into a strip use a mini heart cutter to cut out a heart-shape from each scallop, then stick the frill to the cake just above the coloured frill.

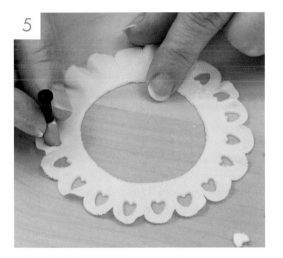

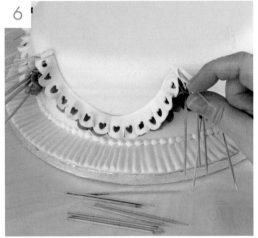

**6.** Leave the cocktail sticks in the cake until the frills are dry, then pull out each stick, twisting it slightly as it's pulled out.

**7.** Pipe a border over the top edge of the frill to neaten it. Use a writing tube (e.g. No. 2) piping tube and royal icing to pipe the design.

49

basic decorations

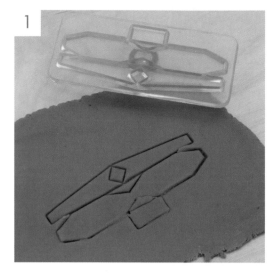

## Classic Bows

A simple way to make bows that are all the same size is to use a bow cutter.

**1.** Roll out some sugarpaste on a surface lightly dusted with icing sugar and use the cutter to cut out the pieces for the bow.

**2.** Take the long strip that will be for the loops of the bow and place it right-side down. Brush a little water in the centre and

then stick on the 2 tail ends of the bow, with the 'V' ends pointing away from the loops. Brush a little water on either end of the loops and bring them into the centre.

**3.** Brush a little water in the centre and then stick the small rectangle around the loops to form the knot in the centre of the bow.

**4.** Pipe a little royal icing on the back of each bow to stick them onto the cake.

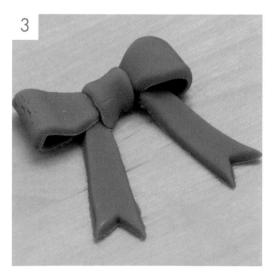

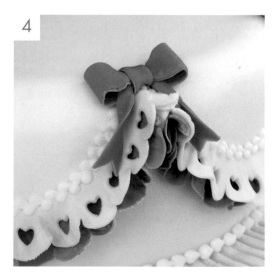

50

# tip

To save time, make small bows from double-faced satin ribbon and use a little royal icing to stick them onto the cake. Make sure any non-edible bows are removed from the cake before it's served.

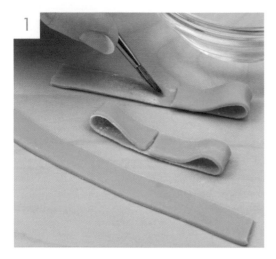

## Round Bows

**1.** Cut 3 equal strips from sugarpaste and bring the ends of each strip into the middle, using a little water to stick them in place.

**2.** Layer the loops up on top of each other in a flower-like shape. Make a ball of sugarpaste and flatten it slightly, then stick this into the middle of the loops to cover the joins.

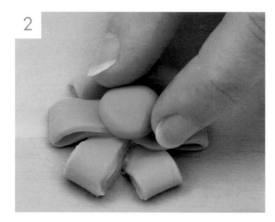

**3.** Brush some water onto the cake under where the bow will be positioned, or pipe on a little royal icing. Slide a palette knife under the bow and lift it onto a cake. It's better to use royal icing to stick the bow on if the bow is already dry, but if the bow is freshly made, then water will be sufficient to glue it in place.

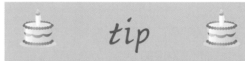

## tip

To save time wrap the cake in real ribbons and stick a ready-made gift bow on top. Using a wide ribbon will help to disguise any flaws in the icing.

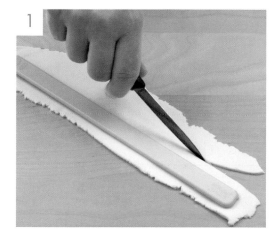

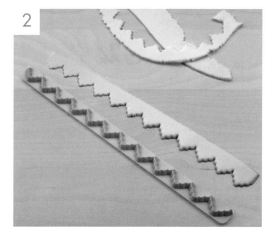

## Straight Frills

As this design is made up from several layers, try to roll each layer out quite thinly otherwise the cake will have a very thick coating of sugarpaste.

**1.** Roll out some sugarpaste and press the straight frill cutter into it. Cut along the base side of it using a knife, leaving just a small gap between the knife and the cutter.

**2.** Remove the cutter and cut the ends to neaten them.

**3.** Paint a line of water around the top of the cake and stick the straight frill so the points are just above the top of the cake.

**4.** Smooth along the bottom cut edge so that there won't be a ridge when the next layer of the frills is attached.

53

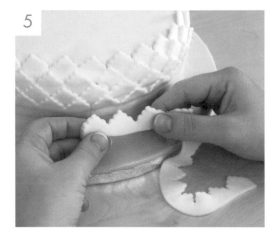

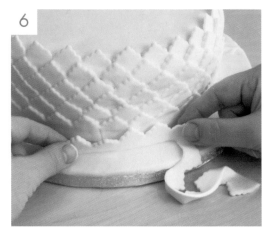

**5.** Build-up the layers of frills, working down the cake. The points will cover any joins in the strips in the layer above them.

**6.** Continue adding layers until the last layer sits on the cake drum. Rub the joins smooth as they won't be hidden on this layer.

## Inscriptions

If it's necessary to put a name or a greeting on a cake, then the easiest way to get even-sized lettering is to use cutters. Roll out some flowerpaste (see page 97) very thinly and cut it into a narrow strip, just wider than the letters to be cut out. Leave the flowerpaste to dry for about a minute and then work down the strip and cut out one letter at a time. Tap the cutter on the work surface to release the letter. If the letters stick in the cutter try letting the flowerpaste dry for a little longer before trying again.

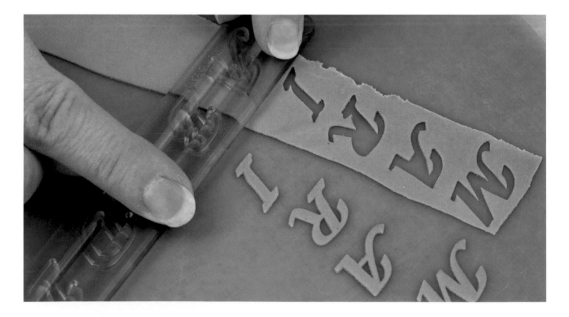

basic decorations

# CHAPTER FIVE

# CHOCOLATE

Rich and indulgent, chocolate is hugely popular with both adults and children. As well as being a favourite for birthday cakes, an elegantly decorated chocolate cake makes an impressive dessert for a dinner party. Many couples are also now choosing to have a chocolate wedding cake rather than a traditional fruit cake.

# Working with Chocolate

Chocolate decorations work well on sponge cakes, and work particularly well on chocolate sponge cakes. There are many different types of chocolate, and generally it's worth paying for good quality chocolate to get the best flavour.

## Chocolate Ganache

Chocolate ganache is delicious and very versatile. It can be used as a thick spreading icing or as a pouring icing, depending on it's temperature. If the ganache is to be used for filling or coating a cake it will need to be well chilled and then whisked until it's light and fluffy before use. For pouring over a cake, the ganache will need to be slightly warm so that it is had a fluid consistency. If it becomes too thick simply re-warm it slightly either in a glass bowl over a saucepan of warm water or in a microwave.

The ganache will keep in the fridge for 3–4 days and then can then be warmed through to use. If it's going to be used to fill a cake and also to pour over the top, pour the mixture into 2 bowls and keep one bowl at room temperature for the pouring and chill the other half of the mixture to be used for filling the cake.

With a layered cake spread a very thin layer of thick ganache over the cake, and then chill the cake. This will seal the cake so that there aren't any lose crumbs when the ganache is poured over. If the cake is chilled it will also help the poured ganache to set quickly.

1

## Making Chocolate Ganache

*Enough to cover and fill a 23 cm (9 in) round cake or 20 cm (8 in) square cake*

450 ml (¾ pint) whipping cream
300 g (10 oz) dark chocolate
Few drops vanilla extract

Pour the cream into a saucepan and bring it to the boil. Break the chocolate into pieces and place them in a bowl, then pour over the boiling cream. Stir the mixture until the chocolate melts, then stir in the vanilla extract to taste.

Leave the ganache to cool until it reaches the desired consistency.

**1.** Place the prepared, chilled cake on a wire rack over a plate. Pour the ganache into a jug, and then pour it over the cake.

**2.** Use a palette knife to spread the ganache out evenly over the sides of the cake. Lift the tray and tap it against the work surface to shake the cake slightly. This will help to ensure a smooth surface, without any knife marks. Leave the cake to set. Any ganache that drips down onto the plate may be strained and re-used.

## Tempering Chocolate

If chocolate is being used to make decorations it is often melted before use and either poured into moulds or shaped as it starts to cool to make decorations such as curls. When chocolate has been melted it

2

chocolate

will crystallise and set as it cools. The crystals form in different ways and tempering is a process that controls the crystal growth to get good results. If chocolate has been tempered properly then it will set quickly with an even, shiny surface and it will have a snap to it when broken. Also, if it's been used in moulds, the tempered chocolate will contract slightly as it sets and will be easy to release from the mould. However, if chocolate is not tempered properly then it will take a long time to set and will remain slightly soft and the surface. It will also have a matt rather than a glossy appearance and may have white streaks in it. There are various methods of tempering chocolate, but one of the easiest is the 'seeding' method. This involves adding some chopped tempered chocolate to the melted chocolate to help the right form of crystals to develop.

**1.** Melt two thirds of the quantity of chocolate. Finely chop the remaining chocolate and then stir it into the melted chocolate to 'seed' the melted chocolate. Stir until all the chocolate has melted.

**2.** Dip the end of a knife into the chocolate to check if it's tempered properly. If it is tempered correctly it will set very quickly. If it's not tempered, then stir in a little more chopped chocolate and test again.

## Chocolate Curls

Chocolate curls look pretty stuck around the sides of a chocolate cake that has been covered in poured ganache.

**1.** Pour the melted tempered chocolate onto a marble or granite board or work surface and spread thinly using a palette knife.

**2.** When the chocolate has started to set use a triangular scraper, such as a paint scraper,

to neaten the edges to give a rectangle that is narrower than the scraper. Clean the scraper so that there isn't any chocolate stuck on it.

**3.** The curls need to be made quickly before the chocolate sets completely. Start at one end of the rectangle and place the scraper just in from the end, and the push the chocolate towards the end, so that it curls. Roll the curls along the board.

**4.** The curls may be stuck around the sides of a cake that has been covered with chocolate ganache. Wear gloves to avoid getting finger marks on the curls.

## tip

If you are short of time stick chocolate-covered finger biscuits around the cake instead of making chocolate curls.

## Quick Chocolate Stars

If you need to make chocolate decorations in a hurry and don't have time to temper chocolate, try using chocolate-flavoured cake covering. The covering doesn't need tempering – just melt it and it's ready to use. To make the stars fill a disposable piping bag with melted plain chocolate flavour cake covering. Cut off the end of the bag to give a small hole and pipe the outline of stars onto a board that is lined with baking parchment. Leave the chocolate to set. (Placing the board in a fridge may speed up the setting.)

Fill a disposable piping bag with melted white chocolate flavour cake covering and cut off the end of the bag to give a hole. Pipe the chocolate into the centres of the stars using small circular movements to fill in the area. Leave the chocolate to set. Slide a palette knife under the stars to release them from the baking parchment. Turn the stars over before use – the underneath is likely to be the better-looking side and should face towards the front of the cake.

chocolate

## Modelling Chocolate

It's possible to buy chocolate pastes which can be used for modelling to make flowers or figures, but it's also very easy to make a paste using chocolate and golden syrup.

Weigh the chocolate you are using and then melt it in a bowl over a saucepan of gently simmering water or in a microwave. Stir in half the weight of golden syrup. For example, if you are using 200 g (7 oz) chocolate, you will need to add 100 g (3½ oz) golden syrup. Stir until the mixture is well blended, then spoon the mixture into a plastic bag and chill it until it's firm. The paste may be stored in the fridge for up to 2 weeks.

## Chocolate Roses

Knead the chocolate modelling paste to soften it before using. If it becomes too soft, return it to the fridge until it is of the right consistency.

**1.** Make a cone-shape out of the modelling paste and press the flat end against the work surface. Take 3 balls of modelling paste and flatten them out into petal shapes. Wrap one petal tightly around the cone.

**2.** Take another petal and wrap it around the first petal. Place the 3rd petal opposite the 2nd petal.

**3.** Press the petals at the base.

**4.** Shape a further 3 petals and then position these evenly around the flower.

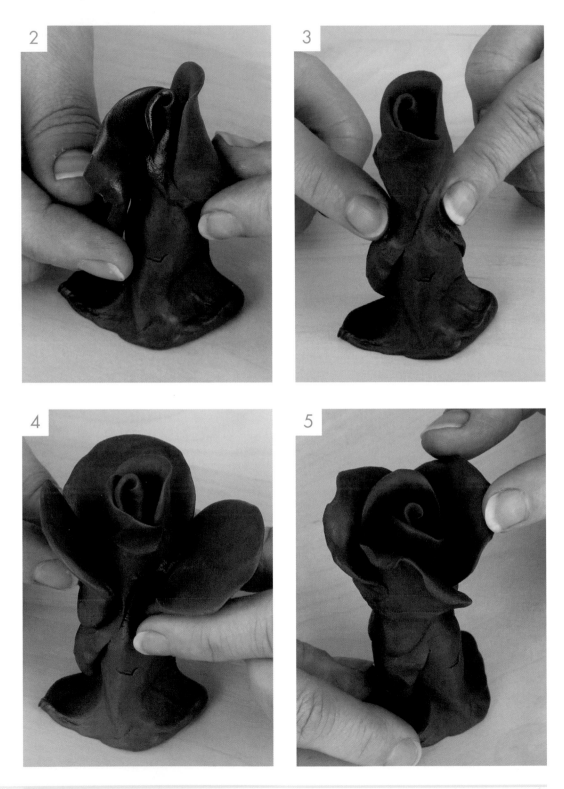

chocolate

If you don't have a silicone veiner simply vein the leaves by pressing the back of a small knife into the modelling paste.

7

**5.** Pinch back the edges of the petals.

**6.** Use a small knife to cut the flower away from the base.

**7.** To make the leaves, roll out some of the modelling paste. Use rose leaf cutters to cut out the leaf shapes. Press the leaves between a silicone rose leaf veiner to emboss them.

**8.** The flowers and leaves may be coloured with a metallic lustre dust or a special metallic powder, such as Moonbeams, which can be brushed on using a dry paintbrush.

## tip

Rather than modelling shapes by hand, look out for moulds made from food-grade silicone. Knead the modelling chocolate to soften it and then press it firmly into a mould. Cut off any excess using a small knife and turn the figure out of the mould.

For really quick-and-easy cake decorations buy ready-made chocolate shapes. Chocolate roses are available in dark, milk and white chocolate varieties and can be used as they are or dusted with lustre colour.

# CHAPTER SIX

# MODELLING

Moulded figures not only add an extra dimension to a celebration cake, they can also be saved as a reminder of the occasion. It's fun to get children to help decorate their own cakes, particularly when making moulded decorations to go on the top of cakes. A fun activity at a birthday party is for each child to make their own figure to place on the cake or to take home with them.

# Making Models

The figures in this chapter can be moulded using sugarpaste or marzipan. Sugarpaste dries out very quickly, so when it's not being used keep the paste well-wrapped in a plastic bag. To stick sugarpaste pieces together brush a little water over the areas to be joined and then press them together.

Marzipan doesn't crust over and dry out as quickly as sugarpaste, but should still be stored wrapped in plastic to keep it fresh and soft. Any pieces made from marzipan should stick together on their own when pressed together, and it's not necessary to brush them with water. However this only works while the marzipan is still soft so pieces should be stuck together within a few minutes of shaping.

## Teddy Bear

**1.** Start by dividing the sugarpaste into a series of balls for making the components. You will need 1 large ball for the body and a slightly smaller ball for the head, then 2 balls for each the legs, arms and ears, which should decrease in size. Rolling balls of paste will help to ensure that pieces meant for identical components, such as arms and legs, are the same size.

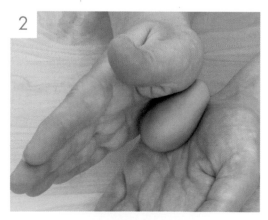

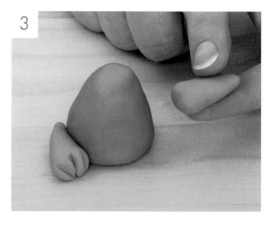

**2.** Make a cone from the largest ball of paste by rubbing the ball between the base of your hands until one end is pointed and the other end bulbous. Press the wide end onto the work surface to flatten it.

**3.** Roll the balls of paste for the legs into narrow cone shapes.

**4.** Use a veining tool to emboss 3 marks on the wide end of each cone, and stick the legs on either side of the body. Make the 2 arms in the same way as the legs and attach them to the top of the body.

**5.** Make a cone shape from the second largest ball of paste for the head, shaping the

narrow end to a point for the nose. Stick the head on top of the body and push the point for the nose up slightly. Flatten the 2 balls of paste for the ears and stick them onto the head, and then press a balling tool into each ear to shape them and help secure them to the head.

**6.** Use a veining tool to mark the mouth.

**7.** Pipe finishing details onto the bear using royal icing and writing piping tubes (e.g. No. 2). Use white royal icing in the eye sockets and then pipe on dark brown pupils and a dark brown nose.

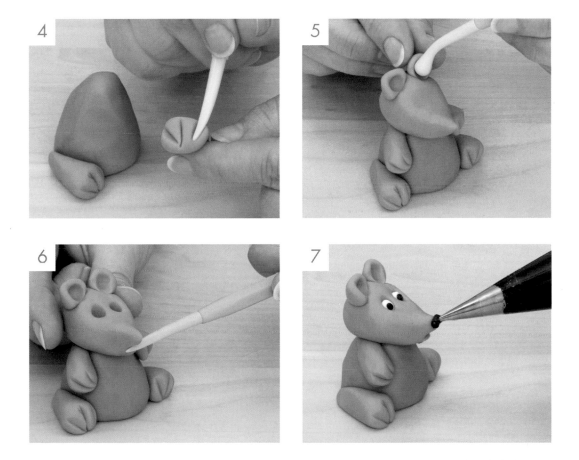

71

modelling

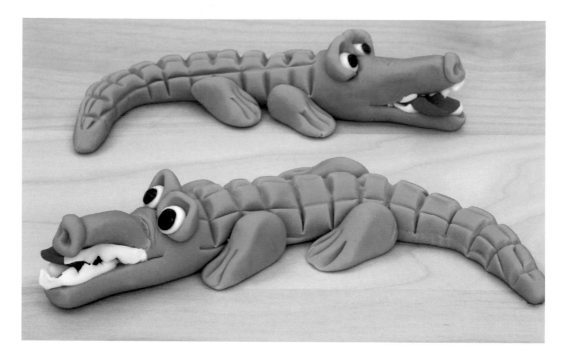

## Crocodile

**1.** Roll a long tapered sausage shape in green sugarpaste, leaving a slightly rounded area for head, and narrowing to a point for the tail.

**2.** Cut into the rounded end for the mouth

**3.** Shape 2 balls of paste, flatten them and stick them onto the head for the eyes. Use a balling tool to shape the eyes.

**4.** Use a veining tool to mark the pattern all the way down the back of the body and tail, embossing it lengthways and widthways to give the square ridged effect.

**5.** To make the legs, take 4 balls of paste and flatten them into rounds, pinching the base of each to make the feet. Using a veining tool emboss 3 lines into each food, then stick 2 feet on either side of the crocodile.

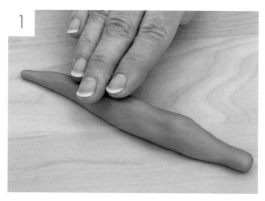

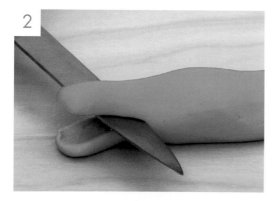

modelling

**3**

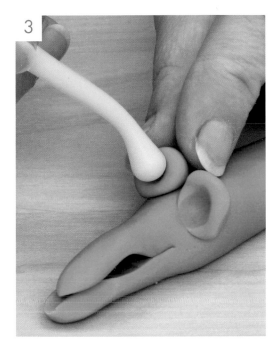

**4**

**5**

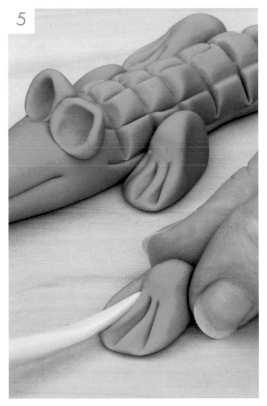

 *tip*

The best method of colouring sugarpaste
or marzipan is to use concentrated paste
food colourings. Add a little at a time and
knead the sugarpaste or marzipan until
you have achieved the desired colour.
Don't be tempted to use liquid colourings
as these have a tendency to make the
pastes go soft and sticky, making them
diffucult to shape.

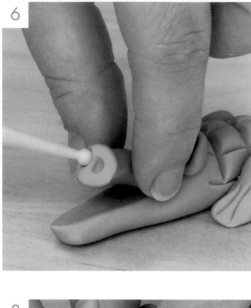

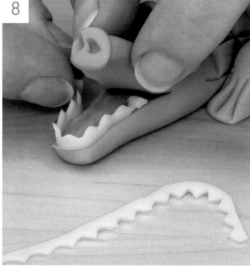

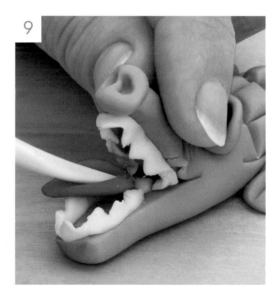

**6.** Shape a small ball of paste and flatten it to make a snout. Stick the snout onto the end of the mouth. Press a small balling tool into the snout to make 2 dimples.

**7.** To make the teeth, thinly roll out some white paste and cut a line using a fluted pastry wheel. Cut either side of the fluted lines with a plain wheel cutter.

**8.** Stick the teeth inside the mouth, on both the top and bottom edges.

**9.** Shape an oval of red paste and flatten it to made the tongue. Press a veining tool into the tongue and stick the tongue into the mouth so that it sticks out slightly on one side.

modelling

**2.** Use a balling tool to make the eye sockets.

**3.** Make 2 cone shapes for the wings and flatten them. Press the pointed ends up into teardrop shapes. Mark 3 lines on each wing using a veining tool and stick the wings onto either side of the body.

## Duck

**1.** Make a cone shape for the body (see page 71) and place the cone on it's side on the work surface. Press the pointed end up slightly to make the tail. Roll a ball for the head. Roll a small cone in orange for the beak and cut it partly in half. Stick the pieces together with the beak between the body and head.

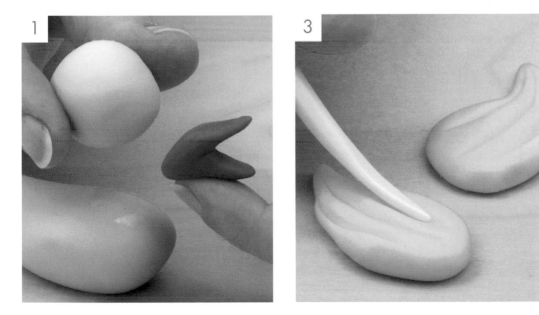

modelling

**4.** Roll a very small teardrop shape to make the comb and stick it onto the top of the head.

**5.** Pipe white royal icing followed by a dark brown royal icing into the eye sockets using a writing piping tube (e.g. No. 2).

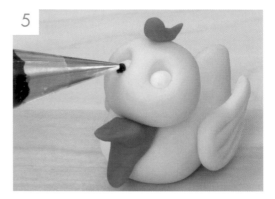

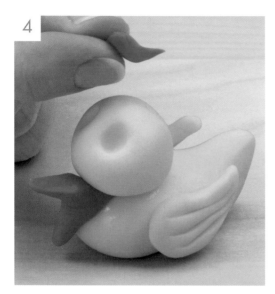

## Freddy Frog (used on cake on page 79)

**1.** Shape a chunky cone shape for the body (see page 71). Make 2 disc shapes for the back legs and flattened at one side to make the feet. Roll a long strip for the front legs. Use a veining tool to mark lines for the feet. Shape a ball for the head and flatten one side of it, then cut into the flattened piece for the mouth. Make 2 small even-sized balls for the eyes.

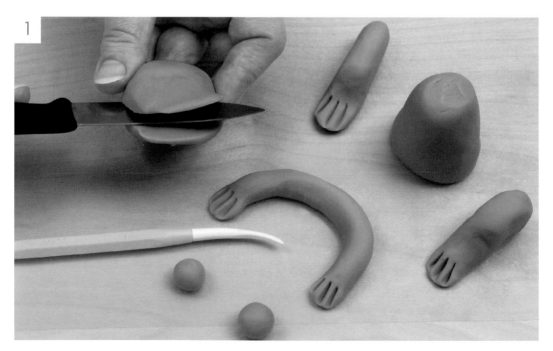

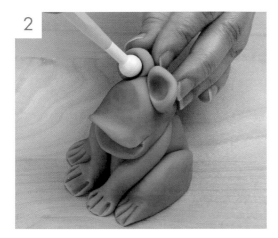

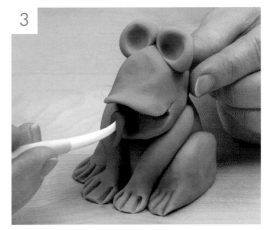

**2.** Stick all the pieces together. Press a balling tool into the eyes to make the eye sockets, which will also help to secure the eyes to the head.

**3.** Take a small piece of red paste and shape it into a long narrow cone. Press a veining tool into the centre of the cone to make the tongue, and while the tongue is still on the veining tool place it inside the mouth.

**4.** Pipe white then black royal icing into the eye sockets, making sure the eyes look in the same direction.

## Clown Fish (used on cake on page 79)

The clown fish is made in white and then painted with the characteristic stripes, so for this model it's better to use sugarpaste rather than marzipan to get a bright white base colour.

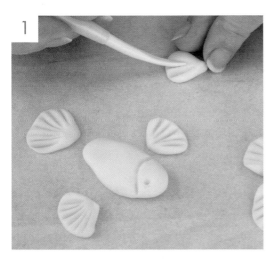

**1.** Make a flattened oval shape for the body. Take small balls of sugarpaste and flatten them for the fins. Mark the fins and face features using a veining tool, then stick them to the underside of the fish.

**2.** Dilute food colourings with water and paint the fish in black and orange stripes, leaving some white areas unpainted as white stripes.

## Starfish (used on cake on page 79)

The starfish is another model that is better made from sugarpaste rather than marzipan, as it's made in white and then painted and sugarpaste has a smoother surface to paint.

Take a ball of sugarpaste and flatten it out, leaving a bump in the middle of it. Place a calyx cutter over the top, with the bump in the middle of the cutter. Remove the star shape from the cutter and use a small balling tool to press into the surface, covering it with small impressions. Dilute food colouring with water and paint the starfish so that some of the colour runs into the impressions to highlight them.

modelling

# CHAPTER SEVEN

# CAKES FOR CHILDREN

Bright and colourful cakes are usually the most popular designs for children. Try adapting a design to fit in with their likes – for example, the castle design can easily be made into a fort with cowboy figures, or if it's made in delicate colours then it can become a fairy castle. All that's needed is a little imagination!

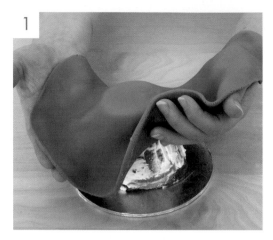

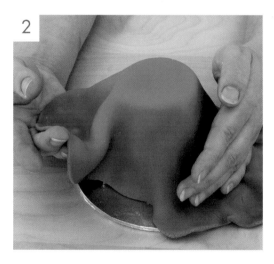

# Decorating Children's Cakes

Children love cakes, and a birthday party wouldn't be complete without a home-made birthday cake. With these fun designs there's something for every child of every age, whatever the occasion. Some of the decorations may look more challenging but with due care and attention you'll be amazed at what you can achieve and the lucky recipient will be delighted with the result.

## Funky Flowerpot Cake

**1.** Bake a sponge cake in a flowerpot and upturn it on a board. Cover with a thin layer of buttercream. Roll out some terracotta-colour sugarpaste and lift it over the cake.

**2.** Ease in the fullness of the sugarpaste so that there aren't any creases and trim away excess sugarpaste.

**3.** Turn the cake over so it's the right way up and then cover the top of the cake using a plain round cutter to cut out the sugarpaste.

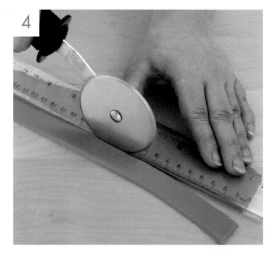

**4.** Roll out some sugarpaste and cut a long strip for the rim of the flowerpot. The easiest way to cut the sugarpaste is to place a ruler on top and then to cut it using a pizza wheel – this will cut through the paste without dragging it.

**5.** Paint some water around the top of the pot and stick the strip in place so it stands slightly higher than the pot.

**6.** Cut the ends of the strip to neaten them.

**7.** Spoon some soft dark brown sugar on the top of the cake as earth.

**8.** Cut about 12 petal shapes from edible wafer paper. It's possible to fold up the paper to cut several petals at the same time to help make sure they are all the same size.

**9.** Pipe a face onto a large sugar lollypop using a tube of ready-made writing icing, or pipe using royal icing.

**10.** Pipe some white royal icing onto the lollypop and stick the petals around to form a flower.

**11.** Stick the handle of the lollypop into the cake.

## Pond Cake (page 79)

The Clown Fish (page 77), Freddy Frog (page 76) and Starfish (page 78) are used to decorate this cake. As there is decoration around the base of this cake, place the cake on a cake drum that is at least 10 cm (4 in) larger than the cake.

**1.** Dot some food colouring over the surface of the buttercream using either the point of a small knife or a cocktail stick. Gently stir the food colouring into the buttercream but don't mix it in completely. Cover the cake with buttercream as shown on pages 29–31, and also cover the top of the cake drum.

cakes for children

85

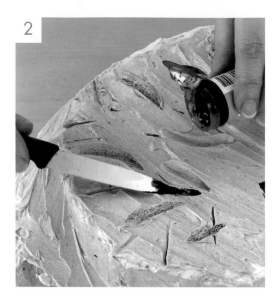

**2.** Once the cake has been covered with buttercream a little extra food colouring may be applied and smoothed over to give an uneven colour.

### Making Coral

The coral is made from Rock Sugar which has been sprayed with red and blue food colouring.

## Rock Sugar

Sunflower oil, for greasing
150 ml (¼ pint) water
500 g (1 lb) granulated sugar
1 rounded tablespoon white royal icing
(see pages 32–33)

Tear off a length of tin foil and brush a thin layer of oil over one side. Use the foil to line a heatproof bowl or cardboard box. Pour the water into a medium saucepan and add the sugar. Dissolve the sugar over a gentle heat, stirring until the sugar has dissolved. Increase the heat and boil rapidly until the mixture reaches 144°C/291°F. Remove the pan from the heat and plunge the base of the pan into a bowl of cold water. Wait about 20 seconds before beating in the royal icing.

**1.** Working quickly, pour the mixture into the foil-lined bowl or box.

**2.** The mixture will initially rise up before collapsing and falling back. Leave the mixture to cool and set.

**3.** When the sugar has cooled brake it into pieces of the required size.

**4.** To make pieces slightly smaller, or to change their shape, rub them against a coarse grater.

**5.** To make the sugar pieces to look like coral spray them with blue and red

food colouring. This can be done with an aerosol food colouring spray, or with an airbrush using liquid food colourings.

**6.** Place pieces of the coral sugar around the base of the cake.

**7.** To make the sponges, shape a small ball of white sugarpaste, then stick some smaller

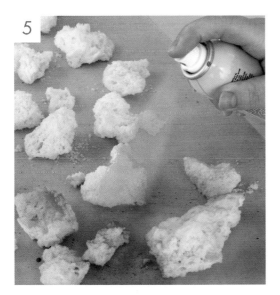

cakes for children

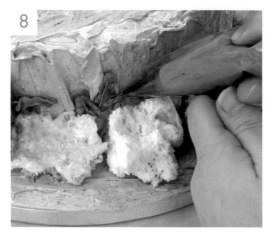

balls of white over it. Press a cone-shaped modelling tool into each of the smaller balls. Paint the sponge with food colouring.

**8.** Pipe green buttercream over the coral and sides of the cake using a leaf piping tube to make the seaweed.

**9.** Place the Clown Fish, Starfish and sponges around the sides of the cake and between the corals. Pipe on any extra seaweed as necessary to fill in any gaps.

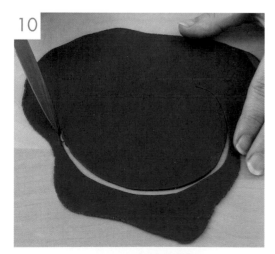

cakes for children

**10.** To make the lily pad roll out some green sugarpaste and use a small knife to cut out a rounded heart shape.

**11.** Use a veining tool to mark veins on the lily leaf.

**12.** Roll over the edge of the leaf with a cocktail stick so that it curls slightly then place the leaf on the top of the cake.

**13.** To make the water lily flowers, place yellow sugar coated chocolates on the cake to make the flower centres. Cut out the petals from edible wafer paper and then stick them around the flower centres.

**14.** Brush a little water onto the base of the frog and then place it on the lily leaf.

 *tip*

Instead of making the fish, decorate the cake with fish-shaped candles instead.

cakes for children

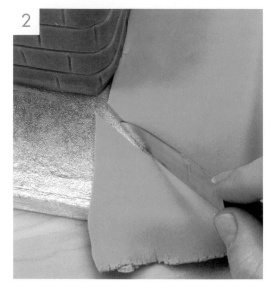

## Cheat's Castle

This cake is easier to make than it looks. The turrets are from a castle cake-making kit and are made from plastic so they just need covering with sugarpaste. The cakes are a 13 cm (5 in) square cake on top of a 20 cm (8 in) square cake. They are stacked in the same way as the wedding cake on pages 112–115. Place the bottom cake on a large enough board to have room for the turrets. The castle cake-making kits come with various size turrets, so make sure the same size are used for each of the 4 corners of each cake, using larger ones on the bottom cake. (The design can easily be adapted and the cake made in feminine colours to make a dreamy fairytale castle for a little girl.)

Look out for plastic figures in a toy shop – knights in shining armour are ideal! It's not cheating to buy them, they become toys to play with after the cake has been eaten.

**1.** Cover the cakes with grey sugarpaste. While the covering is still soft use a veining too to mark on the brickwork (using a ruler will help you to get the lines straight).

**2.** Brush some water over the top of the cake drum and then cover the cake drum with strips of green sugarpaste for the grass, mitring the corners.

**3.** While the green sugarpaste is still soft emboss it using a clean, new nailbrush, twisting the brush slightly to give it an irregular pattern.

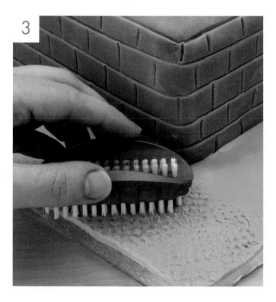

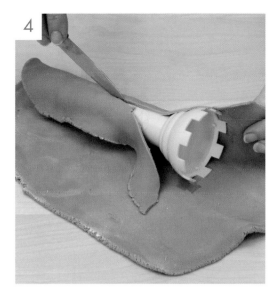

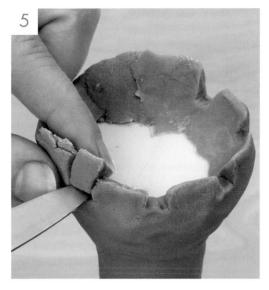

**4.** Roll out some grey sugarpaste. Dampen a plastic turret with water, wrap the sugarpaste around it and trim the sugarpaste to shape.

**5.** Fold the sugarpaste over the turrets at the top, then press the turrets to feel where the ridges are and cut the sugarpaste to shape. Use a veining tool to mark brickwork on the turrets.

**6.** Use a round cutter to cut out discs of sugarpaste to fit inside the top of the turrets.

**7.** Roll out some grey sugarpaste and cut out an arched window shape. Use the veining tool to mark brickwork around it. Cut out a smaller arch shape from black sugarpaste and stick it onto the grey arch, and then brush some water onto the back and stick them onto

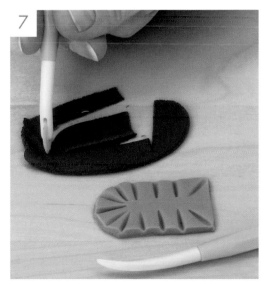

91

the cake while they are still soft so that they will curve around the turrets. Cut out a black arch for the main door, and a brown arch for the drawbridge. Use a veining tool to mark lines on the drawbridge and stick both in place. Use a couple of cocktail sticks as the chains for the drawbridge.

**8.** Make some 'gunge' to stick the turrets by mixing water with sugarpaste until the sugarpaste goes stringy. Transfer the gunge to a disposable piping bag and cut off the end of the bag to give a small hole for piping.

**9.** Pipe some gunge at the corner of each cake and stick the turrets in place.

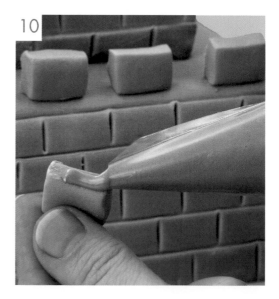

**10.** Cut out some small squares of grey sugarpaste and pipe some gunge onto each and stick them along the top of the cakes as castellation. Arrange the figures on the top of the cake, using a little gunge under them if necessary to hold them upright.

**11.** Cut out paper flags and attach them to cocktail sticks. Stick one flag onto each turret.

*cakes for children*

cakes for children

# CHAPTER EIGHT

# SUGAR FLOWERS

Decorating a cake with flowers adds a pretty, feminine touch. Sugar flowers made by piping royal icing are very quick to make, but if time allows sugar flowers may be moulded from flowerpaste which can look very realistic, and may even be mistaken for real flowers.

## Piped Flowers

Simple flowers can be made using 'drop flower' piping tubes. This type of piping tube comes in various designs for making flowers ranging from simple 5 or 6 petal blossom flowers to daisies with lots of petals. The royal icing may be coloured to the desired shade for the petals and centre using paste food colourings.

**1.** Fill a piping bag fitted with a drop flower piping tube with royal icing. Use a little of the royal icing to stick a piece of baking parchment onto a board. To pipe the flowers, press the piping tube against the paper-lined board and start squeezing out some of the icing. Lift the piping tube up slightly and twist the tube while still piping out the icing, then stop squeezing the piping bag and lift the tube away. Repeat this to make as many flowers as required. Leave the petals to dry.

**2.** Fill a piping bag fitted with a plain writing tube (e.g. No. 2) with royal icing to make the flower centres. Pipe a round dot in the centre of each flower. For daisies, a multi-opening piping tube may be used to pipe a group of dots at the same time,

otherwise with a single piping tube pipe several dots in the centres of the flowers.

**3.** When the flowers are dry then can be lifted off the baking parchment and stuck onto a cake with a little royal icing on the back of each to secure them in place. Alternatively, pipe leaves in green royal icing using a leaf piping tube in the piping bag. As soon as the leaves have been piped the dry flowers may be pressed lightly over the leaves, so that the leaves will hold them in place. If there are any gaps fill in with some extra piped leaves.

# Wired Flowers

Although the wires are not edible, it helps to make the flowers on wires as they are then easy to arrange into beautiful bouquets. It's necessary to use a special type of icing, called flowerpaste, which has gum tragacanth added to it. Gum tragacanth is a powder which makes the paste stretchy so that it can be rolled out very thinly, and also helps the flowers to set hard once they have been made. Most cake decorating supply shops will sell flowerpaste ready made, but if a lot is needed then it's generally cheaper to make it from scratch.

The flowerpaste does dry out very quickly, so keep it well wrapped in a plastic bag when it's not being used. If the paste is too dry to use, then work in a little extra water and some extra white vegetable fat, and if it's too sticky then knead in a little cornflour.

## Making Flowerpaste

500 g (1 lb) icing sugar
10 g (⅓ oz) gum tragacanth
2 tablespoons water
4 leaves gelatine, preferably Platinum grade
30 g (1 oz) white vegetable fat
30 g (1 oz) liquid glucose
1 medium egg white.

**1.** Preheat the oven to 80°C/175°F/ Gas Mark ⅛, or if it's only possible to set the oven to a temperature which is higher than this, then set it to the coolest temperature possible and heat the sugar for less time.

**2.** Tip the icing sugar into a heatproof bowl and stir in the gum tragacanth. Place the bowl in the oven for about 30 minutes, until the sugar feels slightly warm, stirring it occasionally so that it heats evenly. If the oven is hotter than 80°C/175°F/Gas Mark ⅛ then check it more frequently.

**3.** Pour the water into a bowl. Break the gelatine into pieces and add the water.

**4.** Melt the gelatine in a microwave oven, or over a pan of hot water.

**5.** Add the white vegetable fat and liquid glucose and warm gently until the fat has melted. Don't let the mixture boil.

## tip

The best surface to roll out flowerpaste on is a smooth plastic board. Using a coloured board makes it easier to see how thick the paste is and if it needs to be rolled out more thinly. Most boards sold for flower work are made in green. To help make sure that the paste doesn't stick the board may be dusted with a little cornflour. Cut a square from muslin and spoon some cornflour into the centre of it, then gather up the sides and tie with a ribbon to give a small pouch of cornflour, which makes it easy to dust the board.

97

**6.** Tip the warm icing sugar and gum tragacanth into the bowl of a table-top food mixer and then add the melted mixture and the egg white. Beat the paste until it's smooth and stringy. If you don't have a tabletop mixer tip the melted mixture and egg white into the bowl of warm sugar and beat it by hand to bind the ingredients together, and then tip it out onto the work surface and knead it until smooth.

**7.** Spoon the paste into a freezer bag and exclude as much air from the bag as possible. Seal the bag, then store inside another freezer bag inside a plastic container. The paste may be stored in the fridge for up to 2 weeks, ensuring that it remains well sealed. The paste can stay out of the fridge for a few hours while making any flowers, but to keep it fresh for the longest time, it's recommended to store it in the fridge.

The paste may be frozen for up to 1 month. It's useful to divide the paste into 4 bags, and then just one bag can be taken out of the freezer and used as required.

## Wired Roses

These roses are made using a 5-petal blossom cutter. It's easier to work on just one or two flowers at a time, so only roll out small amounts of the flowerpaste as it's needed otherwise it will dry out too quickly. The petals are stuck together with water, which can be brushed on with a regular paintbrush, but using a water brush is even easier as the water is held in the handle of the brush so once it's been filled it's ready to use.

**1.** Using different shades of flowerpaste will help to make the flower look more natural. The full flower is going to have 3 layers of petals, so make 3 different shades of the same

## tip

Wired flowers need to be supported while they dry – if they are placed flat on the work surface then one side of the flowers will be flattened. An inexpensive stand can be made from the a block of the floral foam which is used for dried flower arrangements. Most of the wires sold for sugar flowers have a paper covering, and if they are pushed in and out of the floral foam several times then the paper will start to unravel. To prevent the paper unravelling, press short lengths of plastic drinking straws into the foam, making holes first with a skewer to make it easier to press the straws in. The wire stems of the flowers can then be placed into the straws, rather than sticking them into the foam.

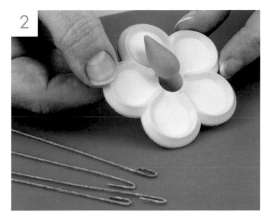

colour. Start by making the darkest colour for the centre of the flower. Save some of this colour, then add an equal quantity of white to the other piece and mix it well to give the colour for the middle layer of petals. Save some of this middle colour and then mix an equal quantity of white with the other piece to give the palest shade.

**2.** Make a cone of the palest shade of flowerpaste, using the blossom cutter as a size guide; the cone should fit within the width of one petal, and should be just over half way the length of a petal from the centre of the cutter. Make just one cone at a time as they need to be soft when they have the wires inserted into them.

**3.** Cut some green 22-guage wires into 3 or 4, and hook over the end of each. Heat the hooked end of the wire until it's very hot in a flame, such as a candle flame or a gas hob. Then insert the hook into the base of the cone of flowerpaste, and press the cone so that it's firmly attached on the end of the wire. The heating of the wire helps to secure the cone as the sugar in the flowerpaste will melt around the hot wire.

**4.** Roll out some of the darkest shade of flowerpaste and cut out just one or 2 sets of petals with the blossom cutter.

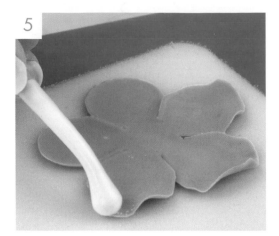

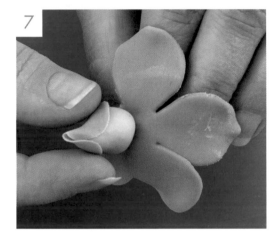

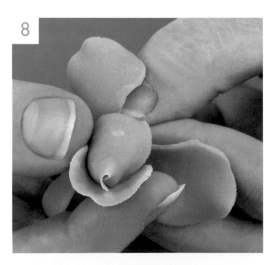

**5.** Place a set of petals on a soft pressure pad and rub over the cut edges of the petal with a modelling tool. Hold the tool so that it is half on and half off the petal and rub gently forwards and backwards around the outline of the petal to give a slightly wavy edge.

**6.** Thread the wire with a cone through the centre of the set of petals. Brush water over one of the petals.

**7.** Lift the dampened petal and wrap it tightly around the cone.

**8.** Dampen the petal that is almost opposite the join of the first petal and then wrap this around the opposite side of the cone.

**9.** Dampen the remaining 3 petals and stick them evenly around the cone.

**10.** Pinch the edges of the 3 petals so that they start to turn back. If 2 layers of petals were cut out, start a 2nd flower.

**11.** Use the middle shade of flower paste, roll it out and cut out another set of petals and soften the edges of them. Brush water on

each petal and then lift them up and position them evenly around the flower, and pinch the edges back slightly.

**12.** The third and final set of petals for the rose is made from the lightest shade of flowerpaste, and is made in the same way as the second set. This final set of petals is positioned so that they alternate with the previous layer, so place each petal centrally over the edge of a petal on the previous layer.

**13.** Pinch back the edges of the petals to make the rose look like it's opening.

101

**14.** The roses can be left with just one set of petals to be a rose bud, or with 2 sets of petals for a medium-size rose. Adding the third set of petals makes them full roses. Pinch whichever is going to be the final layer back a little more than the previous layers.

**15.** To make the calyces, thinly roll out some green flower paste and use a calyx cutter to cut out the shape. To add even more detail, a cutting wheel or small knife may be used to make small cuts along each sepal, but this step may be omitted if the roses are being made in a hurry.

**16.** Pull the wire flower stem through the centre of the calyx, then brush some water over each sepal and stick one sepal up the centre back of each petal.

# tip

When the flower is totally dry some of the cornflour may show on the petals. To remove this hold the flower very briefly in the steam of a just-boiled kettle until the flower is slightly damp, then return the flower to the flower stand and leave it to dry.

16

17

**17.** Shape a small ball of green flowerpaste and pull the stem through the flowerpaste. Brush some water on top of the ball and then stick it to the base of the calyx as the rose hip. Leave the flowers in a flower stand to dry.

Instead of using wires, the cones may be shaped and placed on the end of cocktail sticks. When the flowers are dry the cocktail sticks may be removed. As the flowers are not going to be kept on the end of the sticks, the sticks don't need heating; just stick the clean, dry cocktail stick into the base of the cone and then let them dry. The cones need to dry on the sticks for a few hours before adding the petals, otherwise the flowers may be difficult to handle and may fall off the sticks.

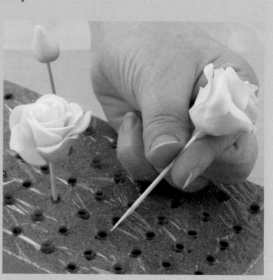

1

## Wired Rose Leaves

**1.** Roll out some green flowerpaste and use a rose leaf cutter to cut out the leaves. Cut some green 28-guage wires into 4. Hold a leaf tightly between the finger and thumb and then press a wire into the leaf, so that it goes just over half-way up the length of the leaf. Make several different sizes of leaf.

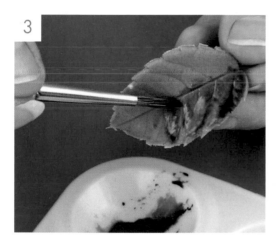

**2.** As soon as it's made place the leaf on a silicone veiner, positioning it so that the wire is in line with the central vein. Press the top of the veiner over it and squeeze it well to emboss the leaf. Remove the leaf from the veiner and twist it slightly then place it in the flower stand to dry.

**3.** Dilute some green food colouring with water and then paint over the top of the leaf, so that the colour runs into the veining to highlight it. Leave the leaf to dry.

**4.** Tape the rose leaves together using floral tape, positioning 2 smaller leaves at the base of a larger leaf.

**1**

*tip*

Adding ribbons to an arrangement of sugar flowers will help to fill in any gaps and add colour. Cut lengths of 28-guage wire. Make 3 or 4 loops from ribbon, put the wire over the centre and twist the wire tightly to secure the loops.

### Unwired Rose Leaves

**1.** If the leaves need to be totally edible, and without wires, then just cut them out and vein the, and curve them slightly before leaving them to dry.

## Colouring Flowers
### Dipping

**1.** Immerse the flower in coloured alcohol.

**2.** Lift the flower out of the alcohol and shake off any excess. Check that all of the petals are coloured, and if there are any bare patches paint on some of the colour using a paintbrush.

**3.** Place the flower in a bowl to contain any splashes and twirl the flower around to spin off any excess colour.

1

## tip

Many food colourings contain glycerine that can soften flowerpaste, and this can be a problem when making dark coloured roses. Making the roses in white and then dipping them into coloured alcohol is one solution for this. Use a 'dipping solution' which is generally available from cake decorating supply stores and which is a food grade isopropyl alcohol. Add liquid food colouring to the alcohol to give the desired colour. Test the colour by dipping a piece of white paste into the alcohol to see if it's the right colour. If the flowers look too pale after dipping them, leave them to dry and re-dip them.

2

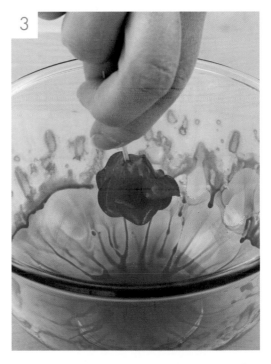

3

sugar flowers

## Dusting

**1.** Use a dry paintbrush to brush blossom tint dusting colour (powdered food colouring) over the flowers that are to be coloured.

**2.** To set the colour, hold the flowers briefly in the steam of a kettle until the flowers look just damp, then remove them and place them on a sheet of baking parchment and leave them to dry.

 *tip*

Making sugar flowers is time consuming, so if you need to decorate a cake in a hurry it's a good idea to buy a ready-made bouquet. However one disadvantage with ready-made flowers is that they are usually only available in a limited range of colours. If a specific colour is required to match your colour scheme then buy white flowers and colour them with blossom tint dusting colour (powdered food colouring) which is available in a huge variety of colours.

# CHAPTER NINE

# WEDDING CAKES

There are many different traditions where wedding cakes are concerned, but most wedding cakes follow the same basic design of several tiers stacked on top of each other. One of the classic photos for the wedding album is the picture of the bride and groom cutting into the cake together.

# Making Wedding Cakes

A tiered wedding cake is a result of customs, superstition and tradition. Wedding cakes are traditionally made from a fruit cake covered in marzipan and royal icing, with the cake stacked on pillars. The icing is white to symbolise purity, and the cutting of the cake represents the newly-wed couple's first role together – to cut their cake share it with their guests. An even older tradition involves the bride cutting the cake and serving it to the groom's family as a symbol of the transfer of her labour from her family to the groom's. There are all sorts of stories, such as if an unmarried female wedding guest takes home a piece of cake and sleeps with it under her pillow she will dream of her future spouse. The top tier of the wedding cake would be saved to use as a Christening cake for the first baby.

However today it's more a case of 'anything goes' and cakes can be traditional in style, in white and ivory, or may be very bright and colourful and a modern work of art. Also any flavour of cake may be used, sometimes with a different flavour for each tier. Mini cakes have also become popular where each guest can take home their own cake as a gift on the day.

## Stacked Cakes

A stacked cake is where the tiers are placed directly on top of each other without any pillars between the layers. If it's a fruit cake then it will be very heavy to lift and may take 2 people to lift it, but it does mean that the finished cake can be transported as it is, and as it doesn't require anyone to set it up on the big day it may be less stressful than having to assemble a tiered cake.

A stacked cake still needs dowels for support, particularly if it's a sponge cake.

Wipe the plastic doweling with an antibacterial detergent and leave them to dry before using them. The bottom tier should be placed on a cake drum that is about 10 cm (4 in) bigger than the cake, and the top of the cake drum should be covered in sugarpaste as shown in Chapter 2.

**1.** For the upper tiers place the cake on the same size cake drum or cake board, then place this on a larger spare cake drum. Cover the cake with marzipan, if using, and then sugarpaste as if the extra cake drum or board is part of the cake, so the board will give support but won't be seen.

**2.** Cut a square out of paper or card to use as a template for positioning the doweling. The doweling needs to be spread out as far as possible, to give support, rather than placing them in just a tiny square. Press one piece of doweling into the cake at the corner of the template. Make sure the doweling is kept vertical and not at an angle and press it down so that it touches the cake drum. Mark the doweling at the top of the sugarpaste.

**3.** Remove the doweling from the cake. For the bottom tier cut the piece of doweling and another 4 pieces so that they are all the same length. It may be possible to cut 2 pieces out of each length of doweling, depending upon the depth of the cake. Press a piece of doweling into the cake at each corner of the square, then insert the last piece of doweling into the middle of the square. The middle tier will only need 4 pieces of doweling, so omit the central one, and prepare the 4 pieces in the same way as for the bottom tier.

**4.** Using the same colour royal icing as the covering on the cake, spread a little of the icing in the centre of the bottom tier, between the doweling. Carefully slide the middle tier off the spare board on top. Check that the cake is level, then stick the top tier on top.

**5.** Pipe a line of royal icing around the base of each cake to fill in any gaps. Before the icing sets, run a finger around each cake to smooth off any excess icing to give a smooth surface.

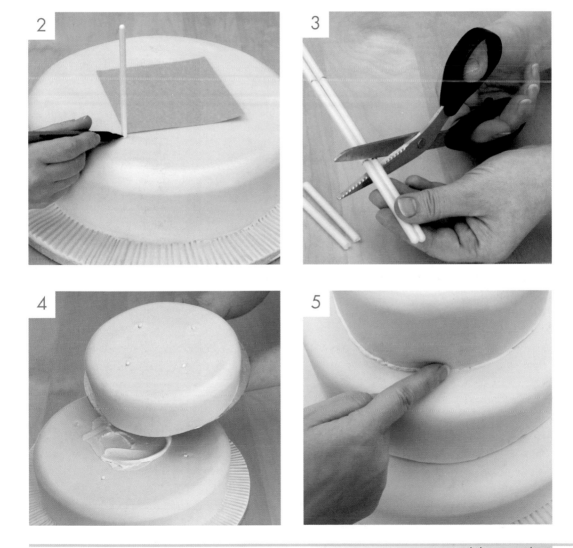

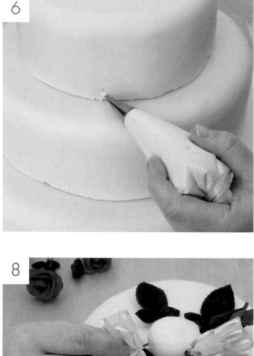

**6.** Pipe a snailstrail (see page 42) around the base of each cake.

**7.** Stick unwired roses and rose leaves (see chapter 8) around the base of each cake. Pipe a little royal icing onto the back of each flower and leaf and stick in place.

**8.** The top of the cake is made using wired roses and leaves and wired bows (see chapter 8). Stick a ball of sugarpaste onto the top of the cake and stick the flowers,

leaves and bows into it before it sets. Cut the wire stems to length, and then stick the components into the sugarpaste, rather like arranging fresh flowers in floral foam. Use ribbons to fill in any spaces so that the ball of sugarpaste isn't seen.

**9.** Pipe groups of 3 dots around the sides of the cake to add some extra decoration.

wedding cakes

## Tiered Cakes

If a wedding cake is going to be stacked on tiers then the principle is very similar when it comes to using dowelling. Usually square cakes have 4 pillars between each tier and round cakes can have 3 or 4 pillars, and it's recommended to make a template for positioning the pillars to get them even. If hollow pillars are being used, then insert a length of doweling into the cake and press it down so that it touches the cake drum. Place a pillar over the top and then mark the doweling level with the top of the pillar. If solid pillars are being used the doweling needs to be cut so that it is level with the top of the cake, exactly as for stacked wedding cakes.

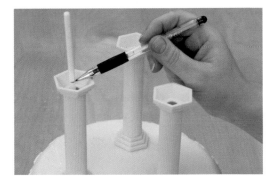

# CHAPTER TEN

# SEASONAL CAKES

Cakes can be decorated to represent seasonal celebrations – classic reds and greens are perfect for winter while bright pastels work well for spring. Flowers can be used to make a pretty Mothers' Day cake and a daffodil design is perfect for a spring celebration.

# Spring Flowers

Different shaped piping tubes can used to create different effects, but the icing may also be textured after it's been piped. For example, brushing soft icing with a paintbrush will change the look of the icing. This technique, called 'Brush Embroidery', is easiest to do in royal icing on a cake that has been covered with sugarpaste.

**1.** To help make all the flowers the same shape use a flower cutter to emboss the surface of a sugarpaste-covered cake while the sugarpaste is still soft.

**2.** Add some piping gel or glycerine to yellow royal icing and fill a piping bag fitted with a writing piping tube (e.g. No. 2). Working on one petal at a time, pipe the outline of the petal and then use a slightly damp paintbrush to brush the icing from the edge into the centre of the flower.

**3.** Using green royal icing and the writing piping tube, pipe stems to the flowers.

**4.** Pipe the long leaves in green royal icing using a leaf-shaped piping tube (e.g. No. ST52). Fold over the ends of some of the leaves to make them look more natural.

**5.** When the yellow petals have dried, pipe a spiral in orange royal icing using the writing piping tube to make the trumpet of the flower.

## Snowflakes

To create a simple yet effective cake design cover a cake completely with royal icing (see page 32–33). Once the cake is covered use a small palette knife to lift the surface of the icing into peaks. Stick the snowflakes into the icing before it sets.

Roll out some flowerpaste (recipe on page 97) on a non-stick board that has been lightly dusted with cornflour. Use a snowflake plunger cutter to cut out the shapes. Press the cutter into the paste and then press down the plunger to emboss the paste, then raise up the plunger. Lift the cutter up, with the snowflake in it and press down the plunger to eject the shape.

## Holly and Ivy (used on cake on page 123)

These leaves are made from flowerpaste (page 97), enabling the paste to be rolled out very thinly. Sugarpaste could be used, but the leaves would be thicker and would not look as elegant on the cake. The leaves can be stuck onto a cake using royal icing.

**1.** Colour some flowerpaste ivory for the ivy leaves and green for the holly leaves. Use embossing-style holly and ivy leaf cutters. Roll out the paste thinly on an non-stick board, dusted with cornflour. Use the cutter to cut out the shape and press the

*tip*

For very quick snowflakes, use decorative punches to stamp the shapes out of white edible wafer paper.

plunger down well to emboss the veining on the leaves. Raise the plunger, and then lift the cutter up. Press the plunger again to release the leaf from the cutter.

**2.** Leave the leaves to dry on a piece of textured foam so that they all dry in different shapes. A piece of crumpled foil may be used if it's not possible to find this type of foam.

**3.** Dilute some food colouring with water and paint some green onto the ivy leaves so they look like variegated leaves, and also paint a deeper green colour onto the holly leaves so that the colour runs into the veining. Allow the leaves to dry.

**4.** Roll small red balls of either flowerpaste or sugarpaste for the holly berries.

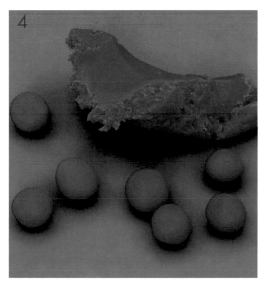

seasonal cakes

# Pinecones

**1.** Shape a ball of brown flowerpaste (recipe on page 97) and make small cone shapes. Place the cones on the end of cocktail sticks and leave them in a flower stand to dry.

**2.** Colour some royal icing to a brown colour and fill a piping bag fitted with a petal piping tube (e.g. No. 58R). With the thin end of the piping tube uppermost, pipe a petal around the top of the cone.

**3.** Pipe a series of small petals in rows, working down the cone all the way to the base. Return the cones on the sticks into the flower stand and leave them to dry. When the royal icing is dry remove the sticks from the cones.

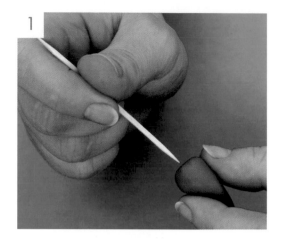

## *tip*

A cheat's way to make pinecones is to take brown sugarpaste, flowerpaste or marzipan and shape it into a cone shape, and then use fine scissors to make lots of small cuts all the way around it.

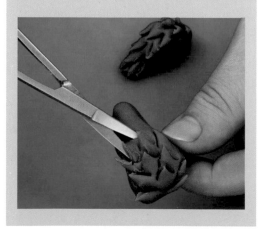

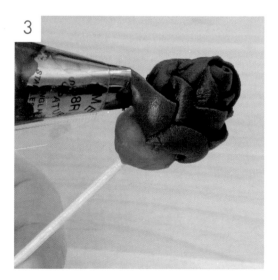

seasonal cakes

# Index

# Suppliers and Useful Addresses

## UK

**Cakedecoration**
Unit 9 & 10
Brember Road
South Harrow
Middlesex
HA2 8AX
England
www.cakedecoration.co.uk

**Squires Kitchen**
Squires House
3 Waverley Lane
Farnham
Surrey
GU9 8BB
England
www.squires-shop.com

**The British Sugarcraft
Guild**
Wellington House
Messeter Place
London SE9 5DP
Tel: 020 8859 6943

## NEW ZEALAND

**Golden Bridge Marketing**
 Wholesale Ltd
8 Te Kea Place
Albany
Auckland
Tel: (09) 415 8777
Website:
 www.goldenbridge.co.nz

**Milly's Kitchen Shop**
273 Ponsonby Road
Ponsonby
Auckland
Tel: (09) 376 1550
www.millyskitchen.co.nz

**Spotlight**
(branches throughout New
 Zealand)
Wairau Park, 19 Link Drive
Glenfield
Auckland

Tel: (09) 444 0220
Website:
 www.spotlightonline.co.nz

## SOUTH AFRICA

**Confectionery
 Extravaganza**
Shop 48, Flora Centre
Ontdekkers Road
Florida, West Rand
1724
Johannesburg
Tel: (011) 672 4766

**Party's, Crafts and Cake
 Decor**
Shop 4, East Rand Mall
Rietfontein Road
Boksburg
1459
Johannesburg
Tel: (011) 823 1988

**Chocolate Den**
Shop 35, Glendower
 Shopping Centre
99 Linksfield Road
Glendower
Edenvale
1609
Johannesburg
Tel: (011) 453 8160

## AUSTRALIA

**Cake Art Supplies**
Kiora Mall
Shop 26 Kiora Rd
MIRANDA
NSW 2228
Tel: (02) 9540 3483

**Cakedeco**
7 Port Phillip Arcade
228 Flinders Street
Melbourne
Tel: (03) 9654 5335

**Cake and Icing Centre**
651 Samford Rd
MITCHELTON
QLD 4053
Tel: (07) 3355 3443

## THE NETHERLANDS

**Planet Cake**
Zuidplein 117
3083 CN Rotterdam
Tel: (010) 290 91 30
Email: info@cake.nl

## SOUTH AMERICA

**Boloarte**
Rua Enes De Souza
35 - Tijuca
Rio de Janeiro
RJ - CEP 20521-210
Brazil

## NORTH AMERICA

**Calijava International
 School**
of Cake Decorating and
 Sugarcraft
19519 Business Center Drive
Northridge
CA 91324
Tel: (818) 718 2707
Website:
 www.cakevisions.com

**Home Cake Artistry Inc.**
1002 North Central
Suite 511
Richardson
TX 75080

**Creative Tools Ltd.**
3 Tannery Court
Richmond Hill
Ontario L4C 7V5
Canada